www.education-punk.de

The ABC's of a
real estate millionaire –
the German way

Dr. Florian Roski
certified building expert,
entrepreneur and real estate investor

"Only if you live it, you can tell it"

For questions, suggestions or further information:
www.education-punk.de

© by Education Punk ltd.
The work, including all its parts, is protected by copyright. Any use not explicitly permitted by copyright law requires the prior consent of the publisher.

Publisher: Education Punk Ltd.
Editing: Iris Lederer, Nürnberg
Translation: Mario Geiss

ISBN Print: 978-3-9817888-4-6
ISBN E-Book: 978-3-9817888-5-3

Contents

Acknowledgements

*my Family: Kathrin & Renate Roski, Elke Holzinger and Tabea Hohbach. Motivator for the translation of the German book "Das 1*1 des Immobilien Millionärs": Mario Geiss.*

About the author

Dr. Florian Roski (born 22.09.1974) is an investor and start-up consultant and lives in Nuremberg. His university education began with a degree in business administration in Nuremberg. After his studies, which he successfully completed as Dipl.-Kfm., he started his practical career in a start-up in the automotive sector, which quickly developed into a system service provider with over 250 employees. During this time, Dr. Roski held various management positions and is still grateful for the lessons he learned from his mentors Mr. Johann Hofer and Mr. Rainer König.
Parallel to his job, he completed a degree in communication science/ psychology, an MBA program with an international orientation and a doctoral program in England. Dr. Roski left this company after nine exciting years and founded four-quarters VAS ltd. Today, under the new name four-quarters EXIST GmbH/ four-quarters Wirtschaftssozietät GmbH, it is the number one when it comes to start-up consulting in Franconia with over 400 foundation projects and 30 colleagues. As it is usual for impatient entrepreneurs, Dr. Roski began early on to take control of the topic retirement provision himself. He is still a passionate real estate investor and has built up his retirement provision over the years by flipping real estate, but primarily by investing in cash flow generating properties, while constantly expanding his knowledge and experience. Dr. Florian Roski is an association-tested building expert for the evaluation of developed and undeveloped properties and works on a voluntary basis for DEGRIN - Begegnung und Bildung in Vielfalt e.V. (meeting and education in diversity).

Dr. Florian Roski knows how to combine entrepreneurship and investment in an elegant way and is one of the most successful consultants in his region. His intention with this book is to explain the topic "Building Wealth Through Real Estate Investing" in a simple and practical way.

Dipl.-Kfm., Dr. Florian Roski, DBA, MBA, M-NLP
Havanna, Cuba

Preface

Since I always try to focus on the essential, I see prefaces as a rather time-consuming and superfluous ballast.

Therefore, you will be spared!

Yet "Motivation", "Acknowledgements" and the chapter "About the author" are parts, which I consider to be important. They give you an impression about the author and why he does write the way he writes and what exactly inspired me to write this book for your real estate success.

I therefore regard transparency as my first duty!

1   Motivation for this book

This book is a system clarifier. It shows how to use a system to build up a fortune with real estate. It does not matter what your current financial situation looks like if you follow all the rules presented in this book.

Although luck may play a role from time to time, it is much more important to do your homework, be patient and detect the right properties. Your success in life is directly proportional to your accumulated knowledge: If your mental vessel grows, then you and thus your success will also grow! My motivation to write this book is to help you to become economically successful with real estate and to finally clear up some myths and misunderstandings about real estate! In my opinion, a non-fiction book only has the right to exist if it provides a clear benefit to the reader. And that is exactly what this book is all about. It should help you to understand the process of purchasing your first property, the financing, the subsequent harvest and the resulting wealth accumulation. I would like to dedicate this book to my students, who never seem to get enough of the topic "Getting rich through real estate".

So, if you are interested in how to build up a large fortune through systematically investing in real estate and how to generate returns of well over 20 percent, you have acquired the right book.

> **Note:** Please read the entire book. Don't skip any chapters. Knowledge is the best insurance against stupid mistakes! And why would you repeat the mistakes I have already made?

Real estate loans are currently at a historically low interest rate level. These low interest rates, resulting in a lower monthly repayment, encourages many buyers these days to accept too high purchase prices. Ten years later, however, at the time of follow-up financing or in the event of a distressed sale, this could turn into a boomerang. Debt should be treated with extreme caution like a loaded weapon to prevent the shot from backfiring. Respect for debt is important!

If you want to become successful in the long run, it is an essential pre-condition to only acquire real estate after rationally analyzing the numbers. We often tend to make our purchasing decisions subconsciouslyand emotionally. We are therefore an easy catch for strong calculators or well-trained salespeople. From now on I will take you by the hand and show you how you can also become a successful real estate investor.

Let's get started!

It has always been my dream to be independent. Wealth and big money as an end in itself are less important to me personally. I don't drive big cars or wear expensive clothes, jewelry or watches. Money has no intrinsic value for me, but it is a tool for enjoying more freedom and independence. And we need this tool to meet our daily needs, to fulfil our consumer desires and to provide a good life for our family. For me, a large property portfolio is the ideal tool for escaping the rat race.

I don't think money itself makes you happy. But I believe that not having enough money leads to a certain degree of dependence and constraints which often make people unhappy. Being financially free means having control over one's own life, having more options to deal with life's adversities and thus being less determined by others; in other words: independence.

Real estate as a retirement provision

Another unpleasant fact is that, due to demographic developments and various political interventions, we will receive less and less statutory pensions in the future. This situation must be compensated by private wealth accumulation. I often hear the argument that you need less money once you become older. I cannot agree to that. When I am on vacation, I spend a lot more money compared to the times when I'm working full-time. I also assume that due to a potential age-related health restriction, you might have to spend more money to generate the same level of life quality as a young and healthy person. This means that if I want to choose between many options even in my old age, I need rather more than less money.

Knowledge makes you a millionaire

Money itself does not make you rich. What makes you rich, is the knowledge about how things work. With the right knowledge, I can build up a fortune again and again, regardless of my current financial situation. This means that if you want to become a successful real estate investor, you must "become smart" first. You've already taken the first step: You bought this book to learn about a system that shows you how to build a sustainable fortune with real estate. Lack of knowledge is the main reason for bad investments in real estate.

This book aims at showing you how to build up a comfortable real estate portfolio, but also how to get started with your first property and what you need to bear in mind when doing so. In a first step, you need to be clear about the direction you want to take.

Note: Only those who know their goal can achieve it!

My recommendation to you: Visualize your goal. Think about what you want to do or buy once you are financially free. Think about how high your monthly net rental income needs to be, so that you can live the life you have always dreamed of. If you set a specific and measurable goal, you will be able to measure your success and see how far you've already come. For example, if your goal is a monthly net rental income of 5,000.00 € you will– assuming that you want to specialize in smaller housing units/ apartments – need 10 paid-off apartments or 20 partially paid-off apartments with an average net rent of 500.00 € per month, to achieve your goal.

Here we go: The property as a cash machine
To turn a property into a cash machine, we should clarify first: What is a cash machine? For me, a cash machine is a system that produces money right from the start without me having to invest a lot of work. By "start" I mean the selection of the right property, the right financing and the selection of a suitable tenant. These three elements must be carefully aligned with each other so that the property can produce money. As with a normal machine, it depends on the correct settings to generate some profits. The secret of "installing" a property as a lucrative investment lies in a simple calculation. All you need is a basic calculator. Adhering to this calculation should be a top priority. My personal favorite is the purchase of a simple apartment. Of course, my approach can also be applied to all

property types. My "sample property" looks as follows. Please don't feel overhelmed by the wealth of information. After reading this book, you will have a clear perspective:

Figure 1: The sample property.

Sample property:
- Two-room apartment
- 66 m² living space
- List price: 99,000.00 €
- Offer without a real estate agent
- Cold rent: 575.00 €/ month
- Non-recoverable incidental costs: 75.00 €/ month
- Recoverable incidental costs: 140.00 €/ month
- Land tax: 900.00 €/ month
- 2nd floor without elevator
- No parking lot/ garage
- Small balcony/ basement storage room
- Well-designed floor plan
- Restroom and bathroom
- General apartment condition: Last restoration 14 years ago
- Gas heating: 7 years old

Building condition:
- Year of construction: 1910
- In an apartment building with 10 housing units
- Architectural style: art nouveau/ sandstone
- No thermal insulation, old building
- No protection of historical monuments
- General building condition: OK
- Maintenance Reserves: 0.00 €
- No renovation backlog
- Last roof renovation: 10 years ago
- Age of windows: 8 years

<table>
<tr><td>

Environment:
- The apartment is in a secondary location
- Good residential infrastructure in the surrounding area
- Well connected to public transport
- In a larger city with at least 500,000 inhabitants in southern Germany
- Positive job and population development expected to be continued until 2030

</td></tr>
</table>

Key performance indicators

To evaluate the success of an investment, the return on investment is used as a performance indicator. The return on investment describes the ratio between receipts and payments of an investment and measures the net income earned within a year as a percentage of the invested amount. The calculated return on investment enables me to measure and compare different investments. The higher the return, the more lucrative the investment. Example: A checking account, which offers an interest rate of one percent on the paid-in capital thus generates a return on investment of one percent per year. Personally, I always use the return on investment of my checking account as a benchmark for alternative investments. Moving back to real estate: Investing in real estate is all about selecting the best objects from a multitude of offers with little expenditure of time. I therefore determine a minimum return on investment as a selection criterion for myself.

Every real estate investor has his own preferences and this minimum return on investment is regularly adjusted due to various factors, such as the current interest rate level for obtaining a property loan or the market demand and supply. The fact is, however, that the higher the return on investment of your property, the faster you build wealth. When searching for a property, my current minimum return on investment, based on the total acquisition costs, is between 6.00 and 700 percent per year. My property should therefore generate a return on investment of at least 6.50 percent. I haven't forgotten that at the beginning of this book I promised you returns of over 20 percent. You have to be patient at this point, as this is just the appetizer. In order not to lose any time in the selection and evaluation process of potential properties, I use a small calculation. With this you can scan the existing real estate offer fast and reliably without losing too much time. All following calculations are based on the purchase of our sample apartment. To better understand my calculation, I have divided it into two steps:

- **Step 1: Calculation of the annual net cold rent**

In the first step I calculate the net cold rent generated by the selected property per year. If the offered property is already rented out, I take a look at the current net rent. If it has not been rented so far, I use common real estate websites to get some information about the net rent of similar objects in a similar location. On the website www.education-punk.de you will find a selection of popular real estate portals that can help you to find suitable rental properties.

In our example the sample apartment is already rented out and the current monthly rent is 575.00 €. Since the incidental costs are divided into "recoverable costs" (expenses to be borne by the tenant) and "non-recoverable costs" (costs to be borne by the landlord), I deduct the non-recoverable incidental costs from the net rent, to receive the monthly net cold rent. Since I am only interested in annual figures when calculating the return on investment, I multiply the net cold rent by twelve (months) and thus receive the annual net cold rent. For our sample apartment, the calculation is as follows:

Object data:
- Cold rent: 575.00 €/ month
- Non-recoverable incidental costs: 75.00 €/ month

Calculation:
01: Cold rent less non-recoverable incidental costs = Net cold rent per month
575.00 € - 75.00 € = 500.00 €

02: Net cold rent per month multiplied by 12 months = Annual net cold rent
500.00 € * 12 months = 6,000.00 €

If I want to calculate the annual net cold rent for a property from the newspaper or online advertisement and neither the monthly cold rent nor the non-recoverable incidental costs are stated in the advertisement, my calculation is based on assumptions (I will introduce these assumptions to you right away) to do a quick check of the property. If the offer proves to be lucrative after this first quick check, I contact the seller, ask for the "correct" data (facts) and repeat my calculation. My presumed monthly net cold rent is the usual rent for an apartment with a similar size in the same area. As "non-recoverable incidental costs" I usually presume 75.00 € for a two-room apartment. This has worked very well for me. If you don't have any experience so far, I recommend you to visit various real estate platforms. After a short time, you get a great feeling for realistic prices and non-recoverable incidental costs. My earnings situation is still reduced by repairs regarding special property and by special levies from the community of owners. When doing a quick check, I simply omit this component for simplification and time reasons. I work accordingly with a higher return expectation in order to compensate for these costs. Finally, with this calculation I want to know what net income the property generates per year, irrespective of interest payments to the bank, special levies and unplanned renovation investments. In our example, the sample property generates an annual net cold rent of 6,000.00 € which is an excellent basis for an initial calculation.

- **Step 2: Calculation of the return on assets**

In order to check whether the selected sample property meets the expected return on investment criterion, we now calculate the return on assets based on the annual net cold rent:

Figure 3: Step 2: Calculation of the return on assets.

Object data:
- Annual net cold rent: 6,000.00 €
- List price: 99,000.00 €
- Maintenance reserves: 0.00 €
- Bavaria - land transfer tax: 3.5%
- Notary costs: 1.6%
- No real estate agent
- Closing costs: 5.1% (Calculation figure 21)

Calculation:
01: List price * 5.1% = Closing costs
99,000.00 € * 5.1% = 5,049.00 €

02: List price plus closing costs = Acquisition costs
99,000.00 € + 5,049.00 € = 104,049.00 €

03: Annual net cold rent / Acquisition costs * 100 = Return on assets
6,000.00 € / 104,049.00 € * 100 = 5.77%

Both agents and sellers sometimes tend to forget about the incidental acquisition costs when calculating the return on investment. The same applies to the non recoverable costs. Without these costs the seller can promote a higher (theoretical) return on investment. However, this type of calculation is simply wrong, as we must pay the incidental acquisition costs (figure 21) when buying a property and we cannot pass on the non-recoverable incidental costs to the tenant either.

Note: Be careful with return on investments calculated by third parties: The calculation method might be different!

Failing to meet the target return

Of course, not every property is suitable for wealth accumulation. Many properties are overpriced, have low returns or simply lack the sustainability we are looking for to build up our wealth consistently. In order to build up your assets, you need to look for properties in which the ratio of acquisition costs to rent is positive. Moreover, it is not so easy to find suitable properties in metropolises with a high demand for living space (e.g. in Munich, Hamburg and Frankfurt).

In our example, the return on assets of the sample property is 5.77 percent. As we are thus below our target return of 6.5 percent, there are three options now:

Figure 4: Options for action if the return target is not met.

Option 1: We try to increase the rent.
Option 2: We reject the deal and proceed with the next offer.
Option 3: We try to renegotiate and squeeze the price until our profitability target is met.

Option 1: Enforcing rent increases can be tricky and might lead to a rift with your tenant. Therefore, I personally do not enjoy this option. Furthermore, I buy a property at the current conditions and not necessarily under the aspect that I still have to negotiate for hours in order to possibly impose a higher rent on the tenant. If the seller thinks that the current rent is too low, then he might increase the rent himself. For the current owner, rent increases are "nice to have", but these are the icing on the cake. Accordingly, the seller's reference to the potential for rent increases is - in my point of view - no justification for a higher sales price. This option is not helpful in the short term.

Option 2: Rejecting the deal is always an alternative if the return target cannot be met. Very important at this point: We do not compromise! A synonym for "compromise" in terms of real estate is "slow asset accumulation" and that is not our goal. So, this option doesn't work either.

Option 3: When **renegotiating**, we do not act like we were in the middle of an oriental bazaar, where each party makes several offers. Instead, we make an oral counteroffer in which we clearly show that we are looking for an investment property. Either the seller accepts the offer because he wants to sell, or we will move on and look for the next potential investment.

Now the question arises: Which price might be appropriate for a counteroffer? This question can be answered by doing the following calculation:

Figure 5: Determination of the target price.

Object data:
- Annual net cold rent: 6000.00 €
- Target return: 6.5%
- Closing costs (CC in %): 5.1%

Calculation:
01: Annual net cold rent / target return * 100 = target price incl. CC
    6,000.00 € / 6.5 * 100 = 92,307.69 €

02: Target price incl. CC / (100 + CC in %) * 100 = target price
    92,307.69 € /105.1 * 100 = 87,828.44 €

The sales price of the seller is unfortunately not your ultimate purchase price. Buying real estate involves further costs such as closing costs. In our example, we assumed closing costs of 5.1%. Keep in mind that this number may vary from case to case. You can find out which closing costs are incurred in detail in "Figure 21: Calculation of acquisition costs". The seller thinks and acts in terms of his list price as he is not obliged to pay the closing costs himself. Accordingly, you should always think in terms of the total acquisition costs (list price plus closing costs).

In our example, with a desired target return of 6.5 percent, considering closing costs and an annual net rent of 6,000.00 €, the upper price limit is around 87,828.44 €. Since the current list price is 99,000.00 €, it is now up to you to place a counteroffer. Patience is the mother of all virtues! It is unlikely that the seller will accept your initial offer right away. This is why persistance and persuasiveness are so important. Of course, you should show some understanding for the seller and his price expectations. This is not about being rude or impolite in any way, you just try to explain your current situation as an investor to the seller, while having a relaxed chat among potential business partners. If the seller is not willing to accept your offer and sells the property to another buyer, you have lost absolutely nothing. The property was simply unsuitable for your wealth accumulation. You just keep looking and congratulate the seller for having found a buyer, who was willing to pay more. However, if it was an investor, he did not hit the jackpot. All I can say is: If I search diligently, I usually make a deal every six to nine months. This is more than enough for a solid wealth accumulation. I never pay more than my calculated target price. If the price is higher, I simply reject the deal by saying "Next, please!" Basically, I don't care about the seller's list price. It just shows me how far apart we are. A property that is below my return target is simply useless for my wealth accumulation. This attitude saves me from wasting too much time on one project if the current price expectations are simply too far away. The rules are simple: Look at as many objects as necessary to find the right one. Use the calculation method mentioned above and with a little practice you will soon be able to analyze a potential object in two to three minutes.

The leverage effect

I promised you returns of 20 percent and more and now I'm talking about overall returns of 6.5 percent. The simple but powerful tool behind returns of 20 percent and more is called the leverage effect, which gets even better with less capital invested.

This effect results, so to speak, from the capital structure of your real estate financing, i.e. from the mix of equity and debt capital. So far, all our calculations were based on the fact that 100 percent of the capital employed is equity. For searching real estate, this is a fast and reliable method to evaluate potential properties within minutes, but in the end we all want to know: What is the return on capital invested? As calculated before, our sample property would generate a 6.5 percent return if we financed it with 100 percent equity; meaning without a loan.

Most people might say now: "My goodness, I would be super glad if I didn't have to take on any debt and could buy this property in cash instead." And I am telling you: "This is the worst you can do!" You would give up on these great returns and slow down your wealth accumulation significantly. And now let me show you in detail what I'm talking about, by using our previous sample property once again. Assume that we would have 17,000.00 € in equity to finance the property. The calculation would look as shown in figure 6 on the following page.

What next? Quite simple: Deduct the interest from the annual net cold rent and you'll receive an annual income of 4,125.00 €. This means that my initial investment of 17,000.00 € will generate a positive cash flow of 4,125.00 € in the first year. This doesn't sound too bad and represents a return of 24.26 percent. But there's still room for improvement! Let's assume that we can convince the bank that the property can also be financed with a lower equity investment, for example 10,000.00 €. This leads to the calculation (figure 7) on the following page.

---

1 For reasons of simplification, the interest rate was calculated on an annual basis and not, as in the case of a fixed-rate mortgage, on a monthly basis. In the case of a fixed-rate mortgage, the total annual interest rate would be reduced even further, resulting in a better return.

Figure 6: Calculation of the return on equity.

Object data:
- Annual net cold rent: 6,000.00 €
- Acquisition costs (renegotiated): 92,000.00 € (incl. closing costs)
- Equity: 17,000.00 €
- Effective loan interest rate: 2.5%

Calculation:
01: Calculation of the loan amount (debt)
    Acquisition costs − equity = total loan (debt)
    92,000.00 € - 17,000.00 € = 75,000.00 €

02: Calculation of annual loan costs
    Loan / 100 * loan interest = Annual loan costs (interest)
    75,000.00 € / 100 * 2.5 = 1,875.00 €/ year[1]

03: Calculation of return on equity
    (Annual net cold rent − loan costs) / equity * 100 = Return on equity
    (6,000.00 € - 1,875.00 €) / 17,000.00 € * 100 = 24.26%

Figure 7: Return on equity with reduced use of equity.

01: Calculation of the loan amount (debt)
    Acquisition costs − equity = total loan (debt)
    92,000.00 € - 10,000.00 € = 82,000.00 €

02: Calculation of annual loan costs
    Loan / 100 * loan interest = Annual loan costs (interest)
    82,000.00 € / 100 * 2.5 = 2,050.00 €/ year

03: Calculation of return on equity
    (Annual net cold rent − loan costs) / equity * 100 = Return on equity
    (6,000.00 € - 2,050.00 €) / 10,000.00 € * 100 = 39.50%

With an equity investment of 10,000.00 € we would receive 3,950.00 € within the first year (6,000.00 € - 2,050.00 €) and thus generate a return of 39.50 percent. If you hadn't known this calculation and I had told you that I generate returns of 35 percent and more with real estate, then you would have probably called me a liar. But as you can see, it is just simple mathematics!

Now let's take it to the extreme! Imagine that you could buy the property without equity or for a symbolic price of one euro. The return would be infinite (without any equity invested) or with one euro of equity investment: (6,000.00 € - 2,299.00 €) / 1 * 100 = 370,100 percent. That means, if I finance the property with one euro, I will receive a cash flow of 3,701.00 € within the first year. That's what I call a cash machine!

To be honest, it's quite hard to finance your first property without any equity. Yet, once you are ready to buy your second or third property it is not uncommon to get a 100% financing, assuming that you have always maintained a good creditworthiness (see chapter "7.1 The bank's perspective as financier").

Simply put, the leverage effect describes the use of capital that is borrowed to make an investment. Accordingly, the return on equity can be increased by a higher use of borrowed capital. Increasing the percentage of borrowed capital works as long as the total return remains higher than the return on your property. In our example, this means that the return on equity can be increased by further borrowing capital as long as the interest rate stays below 6.5 percent. If the loan interest rate were higher, borrowing more would start to reduce my return on equity. In our example, it would therefore make sense to continue replacing equity with borrowed capital from a return perspective. On the other hand, the debt-to-equity ratio is rising with increased borrowing and this also increaes the overall investment risk. In chapter 4 "The three sides of real estate investment" we will discuss the perfect combination of return, liquidity and safety.

Real estate and the potential tax benefit
People often ask me about tax advantages when investing in real estate and I reply: "Yes, they exist! But in my opinion, a potential tax advantage is nothing more than the icing on the cake.

If you buy a property with the goal of building assets, then a potential tax advantage should never be the main reason for your investment. First, every investment has to make sense from an economic perspective and if a tax advantage comes on top, all the better.

Furthermore, the tax advantage resulting from your real estate investment as a private individual is primarly determined by your personal situation. I would like to help you at this point, but I am not a professional tax advisor. Even if, I would need various information from you, such as your other private income situation, your marital status, your preferred financing structure, the amount of rent, and so on, as they all have a significant influence on your tax advantage regarding real estate. Accordingly, I will not even try to simulate your tax advantage in one of my examples.

The advantage can therefore only be calculated individually and not in general. If you want to calculate your tax benefits precisely prior to investing, then I recommend you simulate your tax return with the free tax office software ELSTER. ELSTER offers you an integrated simulation tool that calculates your tax liability quite accurately. Simply calculate your tax return two times; with and without the property. The difference between the two tax calculations shows you the tax effect that your real estate investment would generate. Of course, you can also contact your accountant or tax advisor. Also notice that the property's operating expenses which exceed your rental income can reduce your tax burden. This reduction of your taxable income is called the "tax shield". In practice, I use my personal tax advantage to cover unforeseen costs or special repayments.

Now that we have mastered the ABC's of a real estate millionaire, the question arises as how to proceed with wealth accumulation after the purchase of the first property. As the saying goes, one swallow doesn't make a summer. Or, in terms of real estate, the net cold rent of a single two-room apartment will hardly be sufficient to live a free and independent life.

Accordingly, the next chapter "Systematic wealth accumulation" focuses on this situation and shows you how to develop a system that can be used to further accelerate your wealth accumulation.

If you have already managed to purchase your first property, then I would like to take this opportunity to congratulate you. You are now an official member of the real estate owner community. From now on, you will learn more about managing and controlling your property every single year and this is exactly what you need in order to develop an instinct to make the right decisions. Sustainable success is usually built up in small and solid steps. Overeagerness, on the other hand, only increases the likelihood of making mistakes. If you have difficulties with applying the knowledge from the ABC's of a real estate millionaire and to acquire your first property, then I invite you to contact me and let me help you. It is my personal mission to help people live their professional and financial dreams. My current contact details can be found at www.education-punk.de.

The role of the landlord
As a starting point for further wealth accumulation, we now assume that you have acquired the sample property previously described (see "Figure 1: The sample property"). This property serves as a placeholder and can be replaced by any other property. Put in plain terms, that means: Every year you are now building up equity through your first property. Well, that sounds pretty good. But our goal is to build up a large fortune and not just to buy one single property.

At this point I would recommend you to rest for a moment and not to immediately proceed to the next property. Now is the time to gain experience and to decide how to proceed with your first property. My recommendation: Visit two or three annual meetings of condominium owners. Learn how to submit the incidental cost statement to your tenant and try to make good arrangements with your tenant. Observe your property over a period of two or three years regarding its tax and economic development.

We are now taking a break by settling into the role of a landlord. If you don't have time to prepare your incidental cost statement or documents for the tax office yourself, I recommend using a good accounting firm. You can find my recommendation at: www.education-punk.de. I personally prefer to build up assets that do not consume too much of my time.

Since "we" have opted for a fixed-rate mortgage[2] (more about the topic of financing can be found in chapter 7 "The financing of real estate"), your equity buildup after three years looks as follows:

Figure 8: Equity accumulation after three years.

Object data:

Fixed-rate mortgage:	10-year term
Effective loan interest rate:	2.5%
Monthly annuity:	350.00 € (interest and repayment)
Equity:	17,000.00 €
Total loan (debt):	75,000.00 €

Calculation:

01: Equity accumulation through repayment: Sample period: 3 years

Year	Repayment	Interest	Repayment	Remaining amount
Start				75,000.00 €
Year 1:	4,200.00 €	1,827.09 €	2,372.91 €	72,627.09 €
Year 2:	4,200.00 €	1,767.77 €	2,432.23 €	70,194.86 €
Year 3:	4,200.00 €	1,706.96 €	2,493.04 €	67,701.82 €
Total:	12,600.00 €	5,301.82 €	7,298.18 €	

Equity buildup through repayment: 7,298.18 €

02: Equity buildup through positive cash flow: 3 years

    Annual net cold rent: 6,000.00 € * 3 years = 18,000.00 €

    Loan repayment (annuity): 350.00 € / month * 36 months = 12,600.00 €

    Equity buildup: 18,000.00 € - 12,600.00 € = 5,400.00 €

03: Total equity buildup (3-year period)

    Equity buildup through repayment: 7,298.18 €

    Equity buildup through positive cash flow: 5,400.00 €

    Total equity buildup: 12,698.18 €

Wealth accumulation and cash flow

Put in simple terms, your property has accumulated equity capital of 12.698,18 € for you over the last three years and all you had to do was to combine the right object, tenant and financing structure. The following chapters will explain how this works in detail. This is not a book that wants to remain vague in detail. My goal is to show you a clear and simple way of how to invest in real estate.

Including the initial equity of 17,000.00 €, we would have built up equity of 29,698.18 € after just three years. If you want to understand the calculation of the fixed-rate mortgage mathematically, you can follow the recommendation on my page www.education-punk.de. Here I recommend you various free annuity calculators that I prefer to use myself.

Tax advantages and costs for repairs and maintenance of special and common property were not considered for this calculation. In my personal experience, they cancel each other out if you have not bought a particularly bad property.

Furthermore, you can use the additional cash you've built up for carrying out repairs or modernisations. After three years, we have basically created the following situation:

Figure 9: Asset and cash flow situation after three years.

<table>
<tr><td colspan="2">Assets:</td></tr>
<tr><td>Property:</td><td>One apartment</td></tr>
<tr><td>Acquisition costs:</td><td>92,000.00 € (including closing costs)</td></tr>
<tr><td>Liabilities:</td><td>67,701.82 €</td></tr>
<tr><td>Equity:</td><td>24,298.18 €</td></tr>
<tr><td>Cash assets:</td><td>5,400.00 €</td></tr>
<tr><td colspan="2">
</td></tr>
<tr><td colspan="2">Passive income:</td></tr>
<tr><td>Monthly cash flow:</td><td>5,400.00 / 36 months = 150.00 €</td></tr>
</table>

---

2   In the case of a fixed-rate mortgage, the amount of the monthly repayment to be paid remains constant over the entire agreed term. The interest rate is fixed for the corresponding period. The monthly repayment, also called annuity, consists of repayment and interest. Since the monthly repayment continuously reduces the remaining debt, the interest portion in favor of the repayment portion is continuously reduced.

Monthly cash flow is the monthly surplus that remains after deducting the non-recoverable incidental costs and the loan repayment from the cold rent. This is also referred to as passive income, since rental income is not earned through active work (time/ labor for money). In our example, the positive cash flow over a period of three years resulted in additional cash assets of 5,400.00 €. As long as you rent out your property (without increasing the rent), you will receive 150.00 € per month (or 1,800.00 € per year) without great effort.

Once the loan is repaid, your monthly cash flow will increase by the loan rate to 500.00 € per month (or 3,000.00 € per year). Sounds pretty good, doesn't it? The next task is to find further properties on the market that we acquire, finance and rent out again according to the same system. We repeat this procedure until the desired monthly cash flow is achieved. The good thing about this model is that with each further acquired property, your wealth accumulation gains momentum, as you can see from the following calculation:

Figure 10: Systematic wealth accumulation.

Time	Number of apartments	Cash flow (CF)/ year	Savings (SV)/ year	Equity (incl. CF and SV)
Start		0.00 €	0.00 €	17,000.00 €
3. year	🏠	1,800.00 €	3,600.00 €	40,498.80 €
4. year	🏠🏠	3,600.00 €	3,600.00 €	45,406.46 €
6. year	🏠🏠🏠	5,400.00 €	3,600.00 €	72,302.11 €
8. year	🏠🏠🏠🏠	7,200.00 €	3,600.00 €	108,193.87 €
9. year	🏠🏠🏠🏠🏠	9,000.00 €	3,600.00 €	131,708.34 €
10. year	🏠🏠🏠🏠🏠🏠	10,800.00 €	3,600.00 €	147,003.50 €
15. year	12 * 🏠	21,600.00 €		
20. year	20 * 🏠	36,000.00 €		

Accelerate your wealth accumulation

In this calculation, the entire positive cash flow was saved and then incorporated into the financing as equity for each new acquisition. For reasons of simplification, I assumed that my cash holdings will not bear any interest. In practice, I recommend you to open a checking account which offers attractive interest rates. You can park your currently uninvested capital (positive cash flow plus savings rate) there before investing it into the next property. On my website www.education-punk.de you can have a look at a selection of checking accounts that I prefer to use for my own wealth accumulation. Obviously, you can also use any other account.

You can also use additional equity to further accelerate your asset accumulation. Yet, if you are not in a hurry, it is also possible to stick to your initial investment of around 20 percent of the acquisition costs of your first property, without any additional funds. However, you will rarely get past these additional savings. It is, so to speak, the ticket to building up your assets through real estate and you simply have to buy it by spending the appropriate amount of time and effort. Since you want to invest, I have assumed that you are motivated to save an additional 300.00 € per month for investment purposes. This was the amount which I also saved myself at the beginning to accelerate my wealth accumulation. As I already mentioned: Depending on your other income, you can modify this amount according to your current situation. Accordingly, wealth accumulation takes a little longer or might even be faster.

It is a fact, that accumulating wealth through real estate can be achieved in a structured and systematic way. Another advantage of this asset class is the monthly positive cash flow. Based on the purchase of the sample property and three years of experience, my assumptions in the previous calculation were rather conservative. By using accelerators like special repayments, you can gain momentum even faster.

My calculation was based on the assumption of a normal/ low-income earner who wants to live on the rental income in the long run. After ten years you own more than six apartments with an annual cash flow of 10.800,00 €. Once your six apartments are paid off, your cash flow will increase by the monthly annuities. In our example, your six paid-off properties would generate an annual cash flow of 36,000.00 € (500.00 €

*12 months *6 apartments). This equals a monthly "gross pension" of 3,000.00 €, which means that you receive more than a typical employee from the statutory pension (as of 2018).

In my calculation for systematic wealth creation, I left out all other options that can help to accelerate your wealth accumulation. So, my calculations were still rather conservative. The following figure displays some of the options for further acceleration:

Figure 11: Options to accelerate your wealth accumulation.

- Arrange with your bank for special repayments
- Boost your creditworthiness to get better loan conditions in the future
- Increase your additional monthly savings
- Improve your negotiation skills/ reduce purchase prices
- Rent increases

Accumulate cash

In "Figure 10: Systematic wealth accumulation", I assumed that I always acquire the new properties on January 1 of the year. However, this is an unrealistic assumption. It's obvious that I cannot predict the exact date on which you close your first deal (and the ones after). I also assumed that we would be able to contribute the entire monetary surplus from savings and cash flow payments to the financing in the form of equity or, if required by the bank, offer a property from our portfolio as additional collateral.

Personally, I act rather conservatively and accordingly my own wealth accumulation took somewhat longer than that of people with a lower risk aversion. It took me some time to learn how the real estate business works and I also wanted to be sure that investing in real estate would not endanger my own existence. I think learning how to do it right is a basic prerequisite for becoming successful. If you're heading into the wrong direction, the stupidest thing to do is running even faster. Accordingly, I always tried to accumulate at least 15 to 20 percent equity before closing the next deal. A modest lifestyle and a rising income enabled me to save additional cash and to compensate my loss of speed – resulting from my security-oriented behavior. I can tell you for sure that becoming an investor has made me a much more valuable contact for my clients. The reason for this is that only those who apply what they learned can create real value for their clients. Knowledge itself is rather useless, if it's not applied.

And yes: Saving is no fun and it is incredibly difficult for all of us. I am one of the worst savers. Whenever I have a large amount of money in my bank account, it seems to disappear in a mysterious way for all kinds of useless stuff. Accordingly, I try to reinvest my money quickly so that it is not even available to me for consumption purposes.

For me, safety, but also enough liquidity and a high return are equally important and I do not want to forego any of these components at the expense of another. In the next chapter I will show you how to arrange these seemingly contrary criteria.

I bought my first property in my late twenties. It was a two-room apartment in a block of apartments with about 50 residential and commercial units. The price back then was around 86,000.00 €. The apartment had a small balcony and a parking lot, which I didn't really need, because I had a connection to the subway right in front of the door.

I contacted four banks until I found the one that granted me a loan for this property.

It was then that I realized an intrinsic conflict of goals: I am quite risk-averse, yet I don't want to forego good returns. In the stock market, some might say that this is not a realistic attitude, as high reward often equals high risk. Maybe that is why I have never really succeeded in this asset class. Since I am a risk-averse investor, my real estate investments must follow an orderly pattern to feel comfortable. For me, investing is always about the conflict of objectives between the following components: Return on investment, liquidity and safety. An illustration of this trade-off can be seen in the following figure:

Figure 12: The property-investment-triangle.

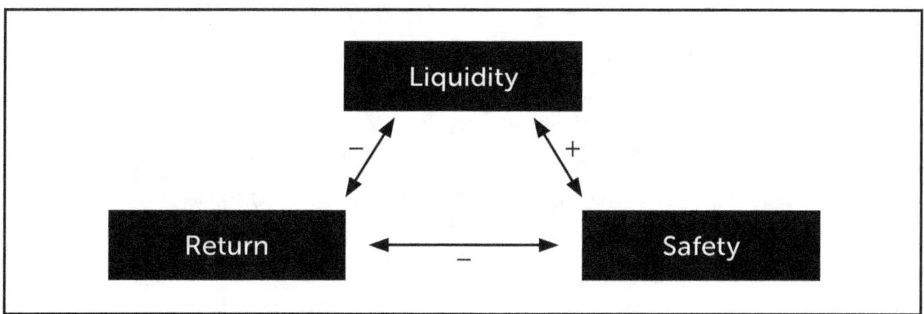

Return on investment, liquidity und safety

Before investing, you should ask yourself the following question: What is my goal with this special object? For me, the answer is simple: I want the maximum return on my capital employed, but also a minimum risk and I want to use as little equity as possible. If a certain percentage of equity is required by the bank, then I want my investment back quickly, so that I am able to use it again for other investments. Can these requirements be met with real estate? The simple answer is: "Yes!" For me and my goals, real estate has become the best asset class I have ever known. Often everything is only a question of one's own horizon. What might be an everyday scene for one person, could be an expedition into new territory for another.

Now, what is the best way of using real estate to get the most out of the combination of return on investment, liquidity and safety? As we have learned in the previous chapters, the return on investment/ earning power of a property is calculated as the ratio between the annual net cold rent and the acquisition costs. Or, in plain terms: How much capital do I invest and what is my return?

You can find the return on investment calculation for our sample property in "Figure 3: Step 2: Calculation of the return on assets" or "Figure 6: Calculation of the return on equity". In terms of earning power, I set a return on assets target of 6.5 percent, which then – assuming an equity contribution of 17,000 € – amounts to a return on equity of 24.26 percent. It goes without saying that significantly higher returns on equity can be generated by reducing the invested equity, as set out in "Figure 7: Return on equity with reduced use of equity". Yet – as you can see from the property-investment-triangle - an increase in the return on equity, which was achieved through a reduction in the use of equity, leads to a relief regarding the initial investment (short-term improvement in the liquidity situation), but subsequently reduces the cash flow sustainably (long-term deterioration in the liquidity situation). In a worst-case scenario the cash flow is even negative. However, a negative cash flow should be avoided whenever possible, as this would mean that you would have to support your investment property with additional liquidity each month. As a result, your liquidity is permanently lowered and the overall risk of the investment increases.

Liquidity is basically the initial invested equity when purchasing a property, but also the monthly cash surplus or deficit resulting from the investment profit from a potential sale. In our calculations we do not consider sales or flips, as we are looking to build wealth through real estate in a long-term-orientied way.

The monthly cash surplus or shortfall is determined by the optimization of the difference between the net cold rent and the repayment. At this point, it is essential to understand, that the financing of your property has to be structured in such a way that you don't have to inject additional liquidty on a regular basis, as the property pays off itself. This approach lowers the risk that in the event of becoming unemployed you will be unable to pay the repayment plus additional costs. The property then operates independently from your current situation without any additional liquidity needed as the repayment is fully covered by the net cold rent. As a result, the tenant pays off the loan himself (through his rent payments). At this point, the property operates like a self-employed worker who is busy building up my assets.

> **Note:** The cash flow of your investment property should always be positive!

Accordingly, you should only increase your return by reducing your equity as long as your cash flow remains positive. If the cash flow is positive, the property is fundamentally independent of your own financial situation and vice versa.

In case of an emergency you can even use the positive cash flow to support yourself financially. The basic idea about investing in real estate in my book is: Build up a high positive cash flow. Furthermore, the debt-to-equity ratio increases with a reduced use of equity, thus increasing the risk of real estate investments. Debt-to-equity ratio is the ratio of borrowed capital to equity. Applied to our sample property, the whole thing looks like this:

Figure 13: The debt-to-equity ratio.

> Debt-to-equity ratio: Debt / Equity
> Example 1: 75,000.00 € / 17,000.00 € = 4.41 debt-to-equity ratio
> Example 2: 82,000.00 € / 10,000.00 € = 8.20 debt-to-equity ratio

The appropriate debt-to-equity ratio

As you can see a reduction of equity increases the debt-to-equity ratio, but also the return on equity increases. The challenge now is to define an appropriate debt-to-equity ratio that represents a justifiable risk.

In general, a debt-to-equity ratio of 4 is considered to be appropriate for a real estate investment. This is achieved by contributing 20 percent of the total acquisition costs in equity. With acquisition costs of 92,000.00 €, the appropriate equity capital input would be 18,400.00 €, as this leads to a debt-of-equity ratio of 4. By comparison, an equity ratio of 33 percent is regarded as ideal for corporate financing. The higher the level of indebtedness, the higher the dependence on financial institutions. It also increases the risk of the creditor, because in the event of insolvency, the sales price of the property may not be sufficient to repay the loan of the property in full. As a rule, a high debt-to-equity ratio also increases the loan rate/annuity and thus reduces the cash flow.

> **Note:** With a positive cash flow, equity should amount to 15 - 20 percent of the total acquisition costs.

A high equity investment (more than 20 percent) reduces the return on equity. However, since the cash flow of the sample property is already positive (see "Figure 15: The cash flow calculation"), a further increased use of equity does not noticeably improve the desired safety and is therefore not necessary.

An equity investment of 100 percent would lead to an ideal cash flow and maximum safety. The return on assets of 6.5 percent would also be good, but not ideal for rapid asset accumulation. Using about 15 - 20 percent equity is ideal for all properties in order to create the best mix possible of safety, return on investment and liquidity/ cash flow.

Determination of the repayment amount

The goal is to generate a high cash flow with an appropriate repayment of the real estate loan at the same time. In practice I prefer repayments of 1.5 – 2.5 percent per year. This means that the monthly loan repayment (annuity) is not too high and a sufficient positive cash flow remains.

Not recommended is an excessive monthly repayment, which causes a negative monthly cash flow. Although you might make good progress in terms of asset accumulation, your risk of not being able to pay the high repayment (e.g. due to illness or unemployment) increases significantly.

Accordingly, it is important to choose the monthly repayment in such a way that on the one hand there is still a good positive cash flow, but on the other hand, the repayment of the loan debt proceeds well.

My favorite form of repayment is the special repayment. Here, I am in agreement with the bank to make annual special repayments of 5 to 10 percent of the total loan amount. Making use of this special repayment is optional and I can freely decide each year how I can use my accumulated liquidity surplus purposefully to optimize my capital accumulation. This gives me the opportunity to choose a rather low regular repayment. In other words: Voluntary savings with high cash flow. That gives me personally the highest safety.

While I'm still employed, I do not need the cash flow, so I use it for special repayments, repairs, special charges, modernizations or the purchase of new objects. In addition, many financial institutions offer annuity loans that allow for changeable repayment repayment during the term of the loan, thus enabling further flexibility for the borrower.

Another benefit of using more equity (i.e. a lower return) is that the monthly cash flow is higher, increasing personal safety and sustainable liquidity. The investment in a property is a system detached from me, i.e. a sure-fire success, which I can feed with further funds, in order to accelerate the accumulation of assets.

Full control over the investment

The good thing about investing in real estate is that I can design all the essential factors such as tenant selection, property selection and financing. This way I have full control over my investment. Control and the possibility of influencing the investment and its essential parameters mean safety. By implication, a high level of risk means that there are hardly any options for influencing the investment.

For me, safety is the key element of any investment. This means I do not like "bad" unexpected surprises that stress or burden me too much. Accordingly, my goal with every project is to reduce all potential risks as much as possible or to think about them in advance and to develop solution strategies. I try to take risk consciously and make it calculable. Risks that I perceived in advance do not bother me. As I've already anticipated them, I've already developed an appropriate solution strategy.

The biggest fears I associate with investing in real estate are: loss of rent over a long period of time, special charges for unplanned expenses on joint ownership or private property, and an unplanned increase in the level of repayments or the situation where I can not repay my loan repayments. Conversely this means that I must find a solution for all these potential risks in advance in order to be in a position where the property operates like a swiss clockwork. To learn more about those strategies, simply keep on reading.

Although the emphasis of my first investment in a two-room apartment was too much on the safety side, it was a good learning example for all following projects regarding how you should not necessarily do it, if you want to focus on a rapid accumulation of assets. The goal is to achieve an optimal balance between liquidity, safety and return on investment/ earning power.

5   Using real estate properly

There is a general opinion that only people who have a higher salary, can afford their own property. This opinion might sound reasonable at first glance, also with regard to the high land and construction costs in Germany. The best way to solve this problem is called saving. This can be achieved in two ways. Firstly, consume less. Secondly, earn more. It may sound simple and the answer is: It is! As the saying goes: "There is no such thing as a free lunch" or as we say in Germany: "Von nichts kommt nichts". Abstaining from consumption, can also be referred to as a negative increase in income. We increase our disposable income by spending less while simultaneously reducing our fixed costs. For most people, daily consumption has become a drug. This drug abuse should be replaced by old virtues. Instead of consumption and instant gratification, we start saving for our long-term fulfillment. A direct increase in income is often the fastest way; e.g. by looking for an additional mini-job. Our stated goal: Building up cash assets of for example, 15,000.00 €. If you manage to save the salary from your mini-job every month and add an extra small part on top, then within three years you will be able to enter the real estate world. After investing our savings, our goal is to generate ongoing rental income. When it comes to the use of real estate, I fundamentally differentiate between three cases: home ownership, real estate flips and cash flow deals. In the following, we will look at all three cases to find out the values of each model for your own asset accumulation.

5.1 The sense and nonsense of home ownership

For many people in Germany, home ownership is considered to be one of the biggest achievements. It is seen as a symbol for a rent-free, self-determined and thus easier life. Yet, if you look at it from an investor's angle, this lifelong dream has little to do with reality. The home generates no rental income, has little tax benefits and claims a high proportion of the monthly net income.

Compared to rents, the homebuyer must pay all administrative and legal costs, maintenance costs that are not ongoing, contributions to the maintenance reserve, repair costs and the cost of money transactions; those are just a few. Owning your home also includes the following obligations: Lawn mowing, hedge trimming, trimming trees, snow removal service, coordination with the chimney sweeper, organizing the maintenance of the house and so on. All these costs, with very few exceptions, must be deducted from the net income. Hence, you will soon realize that it is not all done with the monthly loan repayment. In addition to the development costs for the construction of the house, the municipalities charge additional fees for repairs and additions from the property owners. As a tenant you can see these incurred costs in a relaxed way, because with the monthly rent (cold rent, operating expenses and energy costs), in principle, all costs are covered and capped. In case of a broken heater you simply call the landlord.

In addition, the selection of your own four walls often creates a higher standard and accordingly more money is spent than if you acquire an apartment for renting: In your own four walls, you might prefer real wood parquet or fine stone tiles. Based on the assumption that the tenant saves the free money that he does not lose by buying a property and investing it in the financial market, he often will do much better financially. That is, if a tenant consistently spares his housing cost advantage, he will end up being able to achieve a much higher fortune than a property owner. In addition, the tenant will be exposed to significantly less risk and has a higher flexibility concerning his future plans.

In the usual publications normally only the possibility of renting is compared with that of buying for own use. However, a third option – and in my opinion the best of all three – is usually not even mentioned: rent and purchase leases. This means that you stay in the rented apartment and buy another apartment for investment, which you then rent on. This third option combines the advantages of the other two and, as a result, enables you build up assets significantly faster, without restricting your flexibility.

> **Note:** For the purpose of asset accumulation, your own home is basically unsuitable. It is a liability, not an asset.

5.2 Real estate flips – income profit by sale

There are basically two strategies for making money from real estate: Flipping houses or cash flow deals. By flipping houses your goal is to buy the object as cheap as possible and to sell it at a higher price. Profit arises when the proceeds of sale exceed the purchase price (including any renovation or refurbishment) and transaction costs (incidental and ancillary costs). In a broader sense, transaction costs can be understood as any form of initiation, negotiation, agreement, settlement and termination costs that support the purchase and sale of the property. In the following calculation, the transaction costs consist of the acquisition-related costs, the costs for an ad placement, the costs for the cancellation of a registered mortgage, and the prepayment penalty to the bank.

Figure 14: The profit from real estate flipping.

Selling price of the object: 120,000.00 €
- Purchase price (incl. closing costs): 92,000.00 €
- Ad placement: 200.00 €
- Extinction of third parties rights (notary costs): 200.00 €
- Compensation for early termination to the bank: 7,000.00 €
= Profit from flipping before taxes: 20,600.00 €

In our example calculation, this results in a profit before taxes of € 20,600.00. By flipping real estate, the seller usually hopes to realize a quick profit. Possible reasons for this profit are, for example:
- A purchase price below the usual market price was achieved through negotiating skills and patient object selection. Due to a sales emergency, a good property was purchased at a reasonable price.

- A buying success was achieved in the context of a compulsory auction/ estate administration.
- A property in need of renovation was acquired; through renovation/ refurbishment, a value-enhancing refinement was achieved in the short term.
- Lucky punch; I found a buyer who was willing to pay me a price for the property that was well above the market price.

House flips are always based on the idea of cheap buying with the hope of selling the object at an attractive selling price.

According to my experience, this business model involves a certain degree of speculation (moment of luck) and accordingly requires a higher level of free liquidity in order to be able to finance longer waiting / holding phases, refurbishments or renovations from your own equity. Accordingly, it is not really suitable for the systematic accumulation of assets for persons with limited free liquidity. There are always exceptions to the famous rule. By flipping real estate your goal is to achieve a a high return in the short-term. Accordingly, the risk increases, the safety is reduced and the short-term liquidity requirement increases (see "Figure 12: The property-investment-triangle").

The goal of this book, however, is to enable you to secure assets and to avoid concepts with potential for "bad" surprises. House flips are accordingly only something for experienced and high-liquidity investors. This does not take account of the possibility of being able to dispose of real estate tax-free after a private holding period of 10 years (in Germany, the sales proceeds of a private property after 10 years are currently 100% tax-exempt, limited to 3 properties within 5 years). This should only be used if, firstly, the sales offer is accordingly attractive, i.e. a high tax-free profit can be realized, and secondly, if the gained free liquidity can be invested in new properties. Otherwise, the sale of good assets is rather counterproductive for asset accumulation. Thus, we come to the premier class for the systematic accumulation of assets: the cash flow deals.

5.3 Cash flow deals – buy-to-let properties

In this book, cash flow deals are the investment model par excellence when it comes to the systematic accumulation of assets. Unlike flipping real estate, the focus here is not on the short-term profit intention, but on the sustainable accumulation of assets through regular cash inflows. The cash flow represents the cash flow per period (month or year) and is the result of the cash inflow and outflow, as the following calculation illustrates:

Figure 15: The cash flow calculation.

OBJECT:		123 Main St, Anytown		
		Two-room-apartment		
		Second floor (no elevator)		
		No parking lot/ garage		
Living space:		66	m²	
Year of construction:		1910		
Price/ m²		8.71 €	euros	
Cash flow calculation on a monthly basis:				
Cash inflow:				
Cold rent / Net rent apartment		575.00 €	(66 m² * 8.71 euros)	
Cold rent / Net rent garage		- €		
Total net (cold) rent		**575.00 €**		
Apportionable costs		149.00 €		
Gross rent / cash inflow		**724.00 €**		
Cash outflow				
Apportionable costs:		140.00 €		
Non-apportionable costs:		75.00 €		
Land tax:		9.00 €	%	
Potential rental losses:		14.48 €	2.00 %	
Potential maintenance and repair costs		58.36 €	0.80 %	
			Interest	Repayment
LOAN:		350.00 €	156.25 €	193.75 €
Cash outflow:		**646.84 €**	**156.25 €**	**193.75 €**
Cash flow		**77.16 €**		

A positive cash flow enables the property owner to properly service the loan obligations from rental income, to build up reserves and to make new real estate purchases. It provides information about the viability of the individual real estate business. The current market value of the property plays a minor role for the monthly cash flow. The only thing important to the cash flow deal is the cash flow generated by the property. In the example above " Figure 15: The cash flow calculation "the positive cash flow from this property is 77.16 € per month. In addition to the positive cash flow, the real estate concept is repaying the loan in the amount of 193.75 €. Thus, the property contributes to an asset accumulation of 270.91 € (193.75 € + 77.16 €) per month.

For a cash flow deal, all factors are important which have direct influence on the cash flow in a negative or positive way. These factors are primarily the monthly rent, the non-recoverable costs, the imputed costs and the loan costs. In principle, only a cash flow statement takes cash inflows and outflows into account. Based on the precautionary principle, however, I also consider the possible risk of rental defaults and any maintenance and repair costs, in order to be not surprised by these cost risks. I set up a toll-free money account for these imputed costs myself, which I use to convert part of the rental income into a standing order, so that I can easily cover these expenses in the case of an emergency. In our calculation, these are 72.84 € (14.48 € + 58.36 €) per month.

For me, a risk is only a risk if it is not hedged. Correspondingly, every calculated "risk" is no longer a risk by definition, but a predictable cost component of the business model. In my opinion, there is only a risk if I do not insure these potential expenses with a reserve account. These "ancillary costs" are often underestimated or simply ignored, which then leads to an increased investment risk. In addition, these expenditures occur irregularly in time and in a highly fluctuating amount. After a "good" real estate purchase hardly any maintenance costs occur in the first few years and so it can happen quickly that we simply forget that these expenses exist at all. Accordingly, no liquidity reserves are formed for this eventuality. A good solution, which I can only recommend to you, is to set an imputed average for this type of expenditure from the outset and to set up a reserve account in order to cushion such kinds of costs.

The cash flow statement items that you can significantly influence are the gross rent, the monthly loan repayment, and the choice of the property itself, the composition and amount of recoverable and non-recoverable costs. In addition, as part of the selection process, you can acquire an object that is in a good location and in good condition, so that you can have a correspondingly positive effect on the imputed costs. The composition of these components determines the profitability of your cash flow deal. Since cold rent is the only source of revenue for cash flow deals, it plays a central role. In other words, a residential unit that generates a high gross rent with the same cost structure also generates a higher positive cash flow than the same property with a lower rent. Then the question arises: How can you generate a permanently high (cold) rent? This question is important and at the same time easy to answer: The amount of the rent and thus the value of the housing unit is reflected in the specific way the tenant benefits from the apartment. So, if there are tenants who are willing to pay an apartment rent of 500.00 € for the apartment, then this is also the value that the property has as a cash flow deal for you. For the purchase of cash flow deals, it is accordingly important to acquire residential units that provide a high sustainable benefit for as many tenants as possible. The benefit of an apartment usually results from the location, the condition and the quality of the apartment. Consequently, you can also influence this benefit. For example, by adding a balcony, the attractiveness of the object can be increased. This results in a higher customer benefit and thus the chance of a higher cold rent. This means the value of our cashflow property is rising. However, if I increase the rent of the housing unit without increasing the benefits, then I logically risk that the tenant will move to another apartment in the long term, which will then give him the same benefit at a lower price. The benefits of a property are dependent on many factors, which are often simply summarized under the motto "location, location, location".

Now that the usage concepts of owner-occupancy, real estate flips and cash flow deals have been examined in detail, we are coming now to the purchase of real estate.

This chapter will illustrate how the real estate acquisition for asset accumulation functions. As part of a property check, it shows which selection criteria and documents are decisive for your success and where or how you will find these objects. In addition, this chapter looks at the benefits of real estate agents for the buyer.

The first step: Before you start to look for good cash flow deals, you should in any case make an appointment with your house bank. The aim of this conversation is to define your financing scope. The first step is therefore the question: How much debt capital for the financing of a property would your bank provideand on what terms? This appointment has the purpose that you can adapt your search criteria to these requirements. So, you avoid looking for the "wrong" fruit from the beginning. This saves you time and frustration! Because it is really annoying not to be able to implement a good deal, simply because it is "still" beyond your scope.

> **Note:** Looking for real estate should start with a bank conversation and the question of which financing scope your bank will provide.

It doesn't really matter, whether you actually finance through your house bank or if you prefer another bank. Most banks use similar assessment criteria when lending. Also, it is nowadays common for banks that several offers have to be made prior to getting an order. A decent competition ensures an improved quality of advice, new and innovative products and ensures better financing conditions.
But you should never forget that a good and mutually respectful relationship with your banker will simplify things for you and speed up the financing process. I prefer to do business with people I like and where I am in good hands. Also, the bank talk has another high added value for you. You will learn what is important to your bank and what requirements are specifically placed on you. It's a good idea to ask your financial advisor how you can continue to improve in order to get more leverage in the future.

Consider each appointment with your financial advisor as a valuable consultation and use it to ask all the questions that are important to you and to learn something. When buying real estate for the first time I recommend you to start rather "small", so you decide for a smaller object. This reduces the investment risk right from the start, but has the same learning effect as buying a larger object.

Note: Success comes in small steps!

When looking for good cash flow deals your own attitude is important. Soft as well as hard search factors have to be considered. I recommend you the following procedure: In the first step, you set the funding framework and then determine the appropriate search factors. So, you create a search grid and then start the search. Success in the search for real estate means not compromising, but to search consistently and patiently for the "needle in a haystack". If you can not find a suitable object, then you do not buy one and wait patiently! There is always a chance and the search will qualify you further. With every object inspection you will learn something new and this learning process will improve your real estate education. This often creates new opportunities or interesting contacts. Here, it's also the journey not the destination that counts.

The goal of determining search factors is to develop a search grid that you can use to sort out and evaluate real estate properties. The better you prepared, the faster the object evaluation and the less time you will spend on the search and selection process. The success of a real estate deal depends primarily on the purchase. The quality of your purchase defines the quality of your assets. Accordingly, it is important not to act intuitively and with your heart. It is crucial to the selection process that an investment should always be judged according to the facts. The enemy of facts are decisions based on opinions or assumptions. An assumption in the real estate context is a purchase decision without knowledge and experience or purely based on the statements of the estate agent, seller or other opinion maker. Assumptions always carry the increased risk that they will not occur or are simply wrong. A fact, on the other hand, is a demonstrable or recognized point with a correspondingly reduced risk, that is, a decision based on knowledge or experience. So, whenever I make a decision based on an assumption and not on factual knowledge, I increase the investment risk. Accordingly, the following logical conclusion follows: I listen attentively to all opinions, but I recognize them as what they are: opinions or assumptions. However, as a real estate investor, you prefer the lowest possible information risk, so you simply check all your statements and assumptions. If, you get for example, the verbal information from your realtor, that the additional costs to the apartment amount to 75.00 € per month, then it is helpful for me to make a first quick assessment. But I always ask later on for the housekeeping bills and check this statement. Or if the seller states that the heater is only four years old, then I'll go to the basement or ask for the bill / owner's record showing when the heater was really renewed. I have heard so many false statements in the past that I simply do not accept any more what a seller states in order to protect myself.

I do not want to portray sellers as being bad, but they're just normal people who make mistakes or mistake the numbers. But since I do not want to pay for the mistakes of others, because it's enough to deal with my own mistakes I check everything and reduce my risk of facing false assumptions. Moreover, it is difficult to make the seller or the real estate agent liable afterwards, if individual verbal statements prove to be wrong. The issue of rewinding does not create happiness at any participating party either. Accordingly, in my point of view the responsibility for research rests on the side of the buyer, so that no subsequent disharmonies are generated. The good thing about assuming responsibility is that you have no excuse afterwards or seek your own fault with others. From this perspective, it is always yourself to be blamed if you accept assumptions or statements as facts. This setting usually causes you to automatically check everything you put in front of you to protect yourself from surprises. And that's good!

The German standard notarial purchase contract has a bit of the character of "bought as seen", which many know from the concept of buying a car. Since it is always so beautiful: Bought as seen and trial driven to the exclusion of any warranty. This is the "After me the deluge" - or "What do I care about what I said yesterday" - conception. Accordingly, "check whoever binds forever". Trust only the documents that you have really seen. Often, the number of square footage is extremely optimistic and not really calculated. And of course, the worst neighborhood is the boom district of the future, all the neighbors are always nice and the rent always comes on time.... I hope my message is clear! Accordingly, the purchase of a property is always a bit associated with "exciting" detective work and only good preparation doesn't create any evil, but only positive surprises.

The concept of the search is always: Slow and steady wins the race. This means that you continue to search until you have found an object that fulfills the majority - ideally all - of the desired search criteria. You do not make any bad compromises because you may be impatient and you want to start now. Property search compromises do not usually make you happy, because they are not what we really want. In addition, compromises slow down the successful accumulation of assets.

The cheap purchase is the essential success factor. Accordingly, this should be well thought out. How to search successfully, I'll show you in chapter 6.4 "Searching for the right object". In order to be able to optimally design your search, you should make it clear in the next step what you exactly you are looking for. My recommendation is to focus on a specific category of objects with the aim of becoming an "expert" in this category. It makes sense to select a real estate category that is interesting for the widest possible user layer. Because this category promises consequently, to generate a large demand and a large demand means the chance to achieve a good rental price. Each object category has its own object-immanent advantages and disadvantages. To be an expert in a category is to know as many of these advantages and disadvantages as possible in order to avoid surprises. Basically, the following categories are available for cash flow deals:

- **Commercial property**: The commercial property identifies a building or a building part for exclusively or predominantly commercial purposes. These include production real estate, office real estate, logistics real estate, retail real estate, leisure real estate and special real estate. The difference in comparison to the residential real estate usually consists of a higher investment volume and fewer demands. Commercial leases allow a substantial freedom of contract and accordingly there is no legal tenant protection. There are also differences in terms of treatment in terms of financing, construction law and tax law. Another major problem is the significant dependence of demand on market dynamics and economic developments. Accordingly, as a private investor you should only test this area if you have a high level of expertise.

- **Detached houses**: A single-family home is a building that is usually used by a common house community. One-family houses are classically divided into terraced houses, semi-detached houses and detached single-family homes. Detached houses are usually designed for self-use and less for renting. Since the lot size is unattractive for a traditional property management and the landlord, the acquisition of a family home for investment is only of limited value. Another problem is that property damage - unlike a community of owners - always has to be borne by a landlord alone. This creates work and often expenditures that are too high and difficult to plan. Also, the ratio of space to object is much less favorable than in case of a apartment, which in turn is disadvantageous for tax purposes, since land does not wear out. Accordingly, I would not recommend single-family homes as your primary investment.

- **Vacation property in Germany and abroad**: Vacation property are furnished apartments or houses in Germany or abroad, in which guests can spend their holidays for a certain period against payment. Often these are offered with high return on investment promises (7 to 12 percent). I have only gained negative experience with this form of investment myself and have identified three main problems for which I have not found any solution. Achieving a good return on a vacation property requires good capacity utilization at low operating and repair costs. For this you need, if you do not want to do it yourself, three service providers: a marketing service provider for customer acquisition, a good cleaning and a janitorial service. Often, these services are also offered in a bundle by an operating company. By not usually living close to holiday homes, it is often difficult to verify the quality of these services, which may lead to the following possible issues:

Marketing: Here, the promised visitor numbers are often not generated, resulting in a lower utilization. Since this is a poorly verifiable service, one is, to some extent, forced to trust the marketer. I have not yet experienced a marketer myself who has kept his promises regarding utilization. Also, it can happen that the objects are rented off the books without any knowledge of the owner. Again, a continuous control is difficult. Basically, the risk of fraud is highest when you can not control it yourself. So, there is a high risk in occupancy.

Caretaker and cleaning service: Here, according to experience, often bulbs are changed, and "necessary carpet cleaning" made. Bedding substitute is very often "necessary". In addition to the usual cleaning intervals, very often special cleaning is "necessary", the quality can be extremely bad. Permanent repairs are apparently also "necessary". In direct comparison to a rental, the holiday rental is apparently a business of constant repairs. But you can not test that, unless you live right on the spot and you want to spend your time constantly mimicking the superintendent. The fact is that these services represent a huge permanent cost burden and thus significantly reduce the return.

Customer relations with the holiday home: Here the motto applies: Don't be gentle, it is rental. I have experienced things, nobody believes me. Here, for example, the New Year's Eve fireworks started in the house and not in front of the house and I had to argue afterwards for weeks with the insurance until the damage was replaced. In the case of property damage caused by the tenants, you often get liability insurers, who are becoming increasingly cheekier and are trying to avoid their responsibilities by using a kind of salami tactic. Most of all, I "love" the topic of residual value. For example, your customer has destroyed the floor and you now logically assume that he will pay the cost of the restoration. Wrong thought! The insurance offers you now: You do not get paid the cost of laying a replacement floor, but a "residual value". But for this residual value you do not get a replacement floor, but you have to constantly add something. So, you often have to be enormously tough in order to be reimbursed for the entire costs and that takes time and inner harmony and is no fun at all. Also, kitchen items are often stolen and it also seems to be irrelevant how ugly the things are. So, you have to constantly buy new kitchen items. Accordingly, I can only say that if you do not live at the place of renting or have a different turn to cushion these risks, you should think carefully about whether you really want to face the topic of vacation property. For me, there is nothing better than a good, stress-free and long-lasting tenant-landlord relationship in a cash flow deal. Of course, there are certainly top service providers, with whom the collaboration is fantastic. But I have not met them myself and I have no desire to look for these. I prefer a business that is as stress-free as possible.

- **Multi-family house and apartments:** The multi-family house or apartments in multi-family houses are the asset class of my choice when it comes to the subject of asset accumulation. An apartment building refers to a residential building designed for several tenants. The apartment building may have an owner or may be divided into different owners according to the Housing Act. I do not recommend - even if it should be financially possible — that real estate beginners acquire a whole apartment building. It is better to start your asset accumulation with a 2-room apartment (55 to 75 square meters). Experience shows that this is also a housing size that appeals to the widest demand group. Here can live one to three people. The size of the apartment has little change of tenant, because the living - unlike a 1-bedroom apartment - on this scale is long term comfortable. I myself am not a big friend of 1-bedroom apartments. Although you can realize a higher rent per square meter with these, the frequent tenant change and the resulting transaction costs often reduce the return significantly and generate workload. I like to be stress-free myself. Accordingly, I do not like to buy additional work. Compared to a single-family apartment building, the purchase of an apartment building is more limited in terms of risk, since, for example, repairs to the community property do not have to be carried out by one person alone, but collectively by all the owners.

Accordingly, the risk is reduced. The sole possession of a multi-family apartment building definitely has cost and return on investment advantages, but it requires a higher liquidity stock in order to be able to absorb any damage that may occur. Accordingly, I recommend the systematic acquisition of, for example, 10 apartments, before starting to buy multi-family homes.

In object selection, my personal strategy is to generate as much benefit as possible for a maximum user layer. Correspondingly, over the years, a property search grid - broken down into hard and soft search factors - has emerged, which generates a high level of benefit for the tenant and thus promises a sustainable rental return on investment.

Figure 16: The soft factors.

- Two-room apartment
- 55 - 75 m^2 living space
- Energy certificate positive
- Basement storage room
- Up to third floor no elevator; elevator from the third floor upwards
- Parking lot or garage
- Balcony
- Well-designed floor plan
- Toilet/ bath with window
- Shower and bathtub
- Single-storey- or central gas heating
- Not on a main road (quiet location preferred)

Building condition:

- Year of construction before 1924
- In an apartment building with a maximum of 15 units
- No protection of historical monuments
- General building condition: OK
- Reserves for renewal and replacement: max.
- No renovation backlog
- Roof condition: good
- Age of windows: max. 10 years respectively good condition

Environment:

- The apartment is in a primary or secondary location
- Good residential infrastructure in the surrounding area
- Good public transportation links (metro, bus, train)
- City center is a maximum of 20 minutes away on foot
- City with at least 100,000 inhabitants
- Positive job and population trend

The real estate search is about finding objects that match this search grid as accurately as possible. The more negative deviations, the more the risk of a reduced property return on investment. For example, if the apartment is located on the fourth floor without an elevator or has no bathtub, I may delete elderly, frail or overweight people, people who are comfortable or people who love bathing in a bathtub to relax already from the possible tenant list.

This reduces the benefit of the apartment to a broad demand group and thus the value of the apartment as a cash flow deal. This reduces the cold rent that I can demand for a fourth-floor apartment without a bath. In chapter 6.1 "The object basis-check", the essential points are discussed in detail. In addition, the hard factors are decisive for the cash flow calculation and also take into account the factors capitalization and financing conditions. The following diagram provides an overview of these factors:

Figure 17: The hard factors.

Object data:
- Amount of the net cold rent: 575.00 € / month
- Amount of recoverable costs: 140.00 € / month
- Amount of non-recoverable costs: 75.00 € / month
- Land tax: 9.00 € / month
- No real estate agent
- Land transfer tax: 3.5% Bavaria

Capitalization:
- Equity invested: 17,000.00 €
- Debt: 75,000.00 €

Financing conditions:
- Actual loan costs: 2.5%
- Loan repayment: 3.1%

I receive the property data from the owner or the real estate agent, according to the documents provided. The capitalization describes how much equity is available to me for my cash flow deal. The difference to the acquisition costs is the borrowing requirement, which I then have to finance. The financing terms with which I calculate in the cash flow statement are the result of my bank discussion. In practice, this often results in even smaller deviations in bank terms, as the valuation of properties by the bank also has an influence on the financing conditions. If the detected object corresponds to the search grid with regard to the soft conditions, you make an overall calculation. For this purpose, I have made the following calculation scheme (Figure 18) available to you on the website: www.education-punk.de:

Cash flow calculation on a monthly basis:			
Cash inflow:			
Cold rent / Net rent apartment	575.00 €	(66 m^2 * 8.71 euros)	
Cold rent / Net rent garage	- €		
Total net (cold) rent	**575.00 €**		
Apportionable costs	149.00 €		
Gross rent / cash inflow	**724.00 €**		
Cash outflow			
Apportionable costs:	140.00 €		
Non-apportionable costs:	75.00 €		
Land tax:	9.00 €	%	
Potential rental losses:	14.48 €	2.00 %	
Potential maintenance and repair costs	58.36 €	0.80 %	
		Interest	Repayment
LOAN:	350.00 €	156.25 €	193.75 €
Cash outflow:	**646.84 €**	**156.25 €**	**193.75 €**
Cash flow	**77.16 €**		
Repayment:	3.10 %		
Effective loan costs:	2.50 %		
Overall return without interest:	5.57 %		
Return on equity:	19.12 %		
Object value (acquisition price) nominally:	87,535.68 €		
Real estate agent fees:	- €	0.00 %	
Notary fees:	1,400.57 €	1.60 %	
Land transfer tax:	3,063.75 €	3.50 %	
Acquisition costs:	**92,000.00 €**		
Renovation and refurbishment:	- €		
Acquisition costs incl. R & R:	**92,000.00 €**		
Equity investment:	17,000.00 €		
Borrowed funds (loans)	75,000.00 €		

If the real estate accounts show a positive cash flow, an attractive return on equity and the soft factors allow a sustainable and positive rent development, you can start building your assets by purchasing the property and commissioning a purchase contract with the notary.

In addition to the soft factors, the purchase price and the basic rent of the property are primarily the strategic success factors and decide whether you will succeed with your property in the future. Any reduction in effective cost directly leads to an improvement in the profitability of the property as an investment and vice versa. The same profitability improvement results in a reduction / elimination of the real estate agentage costs. In any case, it pays off to enter a tough negotiation course until the notary's appointment. In the cash flow analysis above, the rent is shown as a static component. In practice, rent increases of up to 1.5 percent per year are possible in attractive cities. In addition to a rent increase, the property is also expected to increase in value. I consider tax advantages, capital appreciation and rent increases rather as the cream on the cake and less as fixed values that I calculate with. Therefore, I act according to the precautionary principle, do not consider these effects and I am happy if the results are better than calculated.

> **Note:** The basic rule for purchasing real estate is: first calculate, then buy.

If you have a penchant for the beautiful, you can really let off steam in the renovation and restauration projects, as long as you don't lose sight of the topics positive cash flow and return. I really enjoy creating beautiful living space.

As you can see from my property search grid for soft factors, I invest primarily in good B cities with population growth and good job drivers. I appreciate Art Nouveau real estate because I am fascinated by their solidity and appearance. I prefer the near-town locations. Mobility is becoming more and more expensive, so people appreciate the subway connection near their apartments. Average price is my segment, because that's what a larger user base can afford. Objects with renovation defects can also be very interesting, because they give you the opportunity to increase the value of an object in the short term with a few skilful manipulations and a little color. These items can often be purchased at a much cheaper price. Private real estate sellers are rarely marketing experts and invest little in paint or flooring to get the best possible price for their property. Also, people often do not have enough imagination for how an apartment can be repainted and upgraded with new flooring. Accordingly, people with good imagination often have better chances of doing good business. The following chapter 7.1 "The Object Base Check" tries to give you a deeper insight into the assessment of the quality of living space and to provide you with support for the selection of your return on investment objects.

6.1 The object basis-check

There are many factors to consider when searching for an object. I am going to explain to you below, which ones are essential for me to so you can use them profitably for your asset accumulation. 15 years ago, the home world was simpler. Either the housing shortage prevailed in Germany or not. Today, both exist in parallel. A surplus of apartments, such as in Hof or Gera, and a lack of apartments, such as in Hamburg, Frankfurt or Munich. Accordingly, a real estate investor today has to consider more factors in order to sustainably enjoy real estate investments:

- **Macro environment / site selection:** An apartment may be "concrete gold" in one location in the world and nothing more than a scrap property in another. How come? The magic word is "demand" and this demand is determined primarily by the demographic situation of a location. In other words: demography is destiny, or the demographic situation of a location determines the fate of your residential property. Demography provides information on birth rates, immigration and emigration, mortality rates, population levels and development. Locations with a high sustainable economic power, low unemployment, good work and training opportunities and high recreational values are preferred by people and vice versa.

> **Note:** Inquire about the demographic situation of a location before you buy a property.

Accordingly, it is important for every real estate investor to invest in regions and cities with positive demographic factors. In addition, I would not necessarily prefer cities or regions that are dominated by only a few companies, such as Wolfsburg or Ingolstadt. As soon as these companies are getting into economic difficulties, the entire region is negatively affected due to their market dominating position. Without jobs, the housing requirement is reduced. Accordingly, I would not invest in regions where military bases are stationed. A withdrawal of the troops is like a clearance command with fatal consequences for the economic space. Of course, you can invest there and not share my "opinion", but why should you put yourself at unnecessary risk, even if it works differently. Even very small towns and villages harbor the risk of the limited demand. Accordingly, I only invest in cities with more than 100,000 inhabitants.

- **Micro environment:** In addition to the choice of location, another central element is the location of the property and the infrastructural connection. In every city there are premium, average and bad locations. The situation significantly affects the purchase price of the property. Good locations are usually characterized by less noise, attractive architecture, green environment or central location. Also, the connection to public transport, shopping and proximity to kindergartens and schools are usually well developed in better locations. As a rule, the center should be reachable in a maximum of 10 to 20 minutes by public transport. A leisurely walk around the target often gives you a quick idea of where you are.

- **The residential building:** Apartments are part of a multiple residential building and thus part of a house and owner community. Well-functioning communities are often recognized by the cleanliness and order, i.e. the condition of the object. Stuffed staircases and cellar corridors, squalid backyards, broken building services, rotten bikes in the bike rack, uncleaned windows, dirty corridors, cobwebs etc usually speak a clear language and should be questioned in any case. They are often - not always - a sign that there are problems in the house community or with individual tenants. Here, attention is needed prior to acquistion to avoid getting involved into a house feud or other problems. Also, I would not recommend properties with more than 15 units or those in which an owner owns more than 50 percent of the apartments. The more units a residential complex has, the less weight the single voice has and the less you can influence the events in your house. Often, small groups form or the property management becomes too power-ful, because owners often do it the easy way and transfer their voting power to the property management company at annual meetings of condominium owners. When an owner owns more than 50 percent of the residential units, he has almost a monopoly on many issues. That does not really make you happy, because in the end you want to be able to contribute with your own ideas.

Of course, I can not go into all construction matters at this point. According-ly, I try to keep it as simple as possible. The areas that can cause major prob-lems and thus expenses are according to experience: roof, heating, staircase, basement, exterior facade and other dilapidations or the overall maintenance status. Here are the following recommendations: Before buying, you should definitely ask about the roof condition and ask when the roof was complete-ly overhauled for the last time. Roofs have a lifetime of 20 to 40 years.
When heating, I recommend you to prioritize gas central or gas floor heat-ing. All other systems are more complicated and often cause problems. For pure electric heaters or oven heaters / night storage heaters I would rather do without the apartment. Unless the price is so outstanding that you have the opportunity to equip the apartment with a new gas floor heating. But it also needs a gas connection! Experience shows that gas heaters have a lifetime of 10 to 15 years.
The younger the roof or the heater, the better and vice versa. Please also take a good look at the staircase, the attic and the cellar, and make sure that you have no water stains or moisture in the house. Water marks are spots with yellow edges and moisture is characterized by mold and a musty smell.

If there is vacancy in the house, you should be careful. A multi-family house in a good location should not have any vacancy unless there are plausible reasons.

Although listed buildings have tax advantages, renovation is often more expensive. Make sure that the house has no renovation backlog. An excellent source of information for all types of dilapidations and deficiencies is the ownership record of the annual meetings of condominium owners. Also, the conversation with the tenant or the neighbors is a good source of information. Just ask the tenant if he is satisfied with the apartment. He has no reason to pull your leg.

Parking possibilities are an advantage. It may be a shame if the situation is bad, but I have never considered it of being a particular disadvantage for renting.

In general, keep your eyes open when buying an apartment. With common sense you can actually get along quite well. If you feel insecure, you always have the opportunity to consult a construction expert before buying and to visit the object with him. Shortcomings often offer the opportunity for further price negotiations. I personally like defects. I prefer so-called "honest apartments" that have many obvious flaws. Then you can easily enforce a price reduction and afterwards remodel the object "new" and at your own choice with the savings. In any case, this is better than an out-of-fashion, but well-maintained property. Price negotiations are often tough here.

Also, I would take distance from apartment buildings, where catering units are on the ground floor. Here you can expect noise and odor nuisance and in the worst case rat visits.

- **Equipment of the apartment:** With the equipment characteristics of an apartment I subdivide myself into "must" features, "target" features and "nice-to-have" features. Must features are features where I do not compromise. If a must is missing, then I will not buy the apartment. Target features, on the other hand, are features that should be present. But if the apartment has other qualities, then you can live without these features. Nice-to-have features are the ones that are not an exclusion criterion for the purchase of the apartment. In the following list I have classified my selection criteria accordingly:

Figure 19: Classification of equipment characteristics.

	Must-have	Favored	Optional
Restroom/ bath with window	■		
Bathtub	■		
Toilet/ bath/ shower available	■		
Well-designed floor plan	■		
Gas heating (Single-storey or central)	■		
Basement storage room	■		
Elevator from the third floor upwards	■		
No ground-floor apartment	■		
Not on a main road	■		
Ceiling height of at least 2.40 m	■		
Bright apartment	■		
No hereditary lease	■		
Balcony/ terrace/ loggia		■	
Shower		■	
Windows in good condition		■	
Bath tiled up to door height		■	
Cable/ satellite connection		■	
Telephone socket		■	
Intercom door opener		■	
Bicycle storage room			■
Parking lot/ garage			■
Thermal insulation			■
Year of construction before 1924			■
Attic room			■
No protection of historical monuments			■
Separate restroom			■
Built-in cupboards			■
Shutters			■

I think most of these features are self-explanatory. One feature, however, I would like to discuss in more detail, since often different views are represented: The floor plan. A good floor plan increases the living comfort, a worse does the opposite. Unfavorable are: walk-through room, a too small kitchen, where there is no room for a small breakfast table, a too large hallway, a too small bathroom, in which you do not feel well. No room should be cut like a tube and be cramped. Ideal are a large living room and a bedroom in which a large bed and a wardrobe have sufficient space. A too large bedroom makes little sense, since the rest of the place usually does not give any further benefits. It is very good if there is a restroom for guests and a bathroom with bathtub and shower. As a result, you now have a first search grid that you can enrich over time with your own experience as a real estate investor.

Another essential element for your successful object selection are the object documents, at which we will now look together.

6.2 Purchasing documents and their importance

Before doing a cash flow deal, you should be well informed about the property and gather as many facts as possible in order to relax the purchase process. The main documents are listed below and briefly explained. Before each purchase, you should therefore request these documents from the real estate seller. A checklist "List of documents for the purchase of real estate" can also be found on my website www.education-punk.de for free download.

- **Abstract of title:** The land register is an official register listing the ownership of land and the charges borne by it. The seller usually has an excerpt from the land register as proof of his ownership. Your task is to study the extract carefully and to check whether the seller really is the owner of the property and whether there are rights on the property or real estate in favor of third parties that are disadvantageous for you.

- **Floor plan (true to scale)/ calculation of residential floor area:** As already stated in the equipment features, a good floor plan is a must. The floor plan calculation shows you how many square meters each room has in detail and the apartment as a whole. I recommend to measure the surface calculation at least randomly on site with a yardstick. You never know!

Figure 20: The list of documents for the purchase of real estate.

■ Abstract of title	■ Status of reserves for renewal and replacement
■ Floor plan (true to scale)	■ Protocol of condiminium owners meetings (for the last three years)
■ Declaration of division	■ Annual statement of the last three years
■ Calculation of residential floor area	■ Rental contract incl. handover certificate
■ Site plan	■ Building plans(-drawings)/Building permit
■ Economic plan	■ Building and equipment specification
■ Energy certificate	■ Proof of property and fire insurance
■ Proof of repairs	■ Land tax assessment
	■ Confirmation of the property management that there are no outstanding payments from the seller

■ **Declaration of division**: The declaration of division divides the "total" ownership of the property into co-ownership shares and defines the residential property and the fractional ownership in detail. The residential property is the property of a single apartment. The ownership of the apartment is established in a land register sheet. The fractional ownership in turn describes the special property of rooms that are not used for residential purposes and is attributed through co-ownership of each residential property. The sum of all co-ownership shares then describes the ownership of the entire object. In addition, there are special rights of use, which certify the right of an owner to use a part of the community property exclusively. These include, for example, garages, loft shares or parking lots. Common property is the land as well as parts, complex and facilities of the building that are no special property or owned by a third party. The subdivision into common and private property determines the cost distribution of the building and should be checked accordingly before the purchase.

- **Site plan:** The site plan is a scale representation of an object in the context of its environment, situation and location. Thus, the map provides information about the relative position of the object and is usually requested by the financial institution for financing.

- **Economic plan:** The economic plan sets out the expected revenue and expenditure for the coming marketing year and, separately, the allocation to the maintenance reserve for the common property. The economic plan is composed of the overall economic plan and the individual economic plans for each condominium. The economic plan is passed in the context of the owners' meeting and establishes the legal obligation of the owners to pay the house fee. In turn, the comdominium fee is made up of a portion of the house community allowance payable to the tenant and a non-recoverable portion of the house community allowance. For example, the real estate transfer tax, administrative costs (incurred by the landlord for the administration of the house), maintenance and repair costs, landlord's bank charges and postage costs for the accounts, depreciation and reserves are non-recoverable. The balance is payable to the tenant and from this in the context of its utility bill to pay. The cost structure of the house community billing should be studied carefully, because this affects the rental return on investment, as well as the amount of incidental costs for the tenant.

- **Annual statement:** The annual statement is the annual comparison of all income and expenses due to the owner community. Furthermore, the annual statement includes the status and development of the maintenance reserve. The annual statement contains a total bill of costs, arranged according to cost types, the distribution key as well as the individual billings for the respective apartment building. The result of each individual bill is either an additional payment or a credit. The recipient of the annual statement - and thus also the creditor or debtor of the additional payment / the credit - is the owner who is registered in the land register at the time of the resolution on the annual statement of account.

> **Note:** In case of purchasing a condominium, the time of the change of ownership in the land register determines who is the addressee and thus the debtor / creditor of the annual statement.

The new owner is not liable for agreed, but unpaid house payments of the previous owner. However, provisions may be made in the community regulations and/ or in the contract of sale which deviate from the statutory provisions.

- **Residuals:** It can happen, of course, that at the time of the purchase of the property there are arrears for unpaid house fees, special charges or arrears from annual accounts. In order to avoid discussions in the aftermath, you can get a confirmation from the property management company before you buy that there are no arrears from the seller. If there are still open positions, one solution will be to include them in the notarised purchase contract, so that these amounts are paid directly by the purchase price payment to the property management.

- **Reserves for renewal and replacement:** The maintenance reserve includes the accumulation of a reasonable amount of money to finance the necessary repairs, maintenance and modernization of the common property. The maintenance reserve is paid proportionately by all co-owners. When selling an apartment, the maintenance reserve is transferred pro rata to the new owner. There is no entitlement to disbursement of the maintenance reserve. When buying an apartment, you should make sure to be informed about the amount of the maintenance reserve and to include this in the notary contract, because it reduces the real estate transfer tax on a pro rata basis. A high maintenance reserve is always cheap for the buyer and vice versa.

- **Protocol of condominium owners meeting:** The owner of the residential property (for example, the apartment building) is obliged to hold a meeting of condominium owners at least once a year. During this meeting, the economic plan, maintenance and repair plans, issues concerning the order and management of the object and so on are discussed. The meeting minutes contain all agenda items as well as the resolutions and voting results. Owner records are a good source of information for the real estate investor, which can provide information about upcoming investments and issues. Before each purchase I always request the owner records of the last three years to check which surprises the object may hold for me.

- **Energy certificate:** The energy certificate is a document that provides information about the energy quality of a house and informs about potential improvements in terms of energy efficiency. The purchaser must be provided with an energy pass immediately upon request. Exceptions to this are small buildings and monuments. The energy certificate is created for the entire building and not for a single condominium.

- **Proof of repairs:** If the seller or real estate agent addresses repairs or modernization plans, I can only recommend one procedure to you: Get copies of all the plans. This protects you from improper illegal work and confirms that these plans have actually been carried out and how and in what quality / price level the work has been carried out. In the best case, there are still individual warranty claims that you are entitled to. In any case, a worthwhile approach!

- **Handover certificate:** The lease is an agreement that governs the provision of an apartment for residential purposes against payment of rent for a certain period of time. Since the introduction of the tenancy law is not the purpose of this book, I recommend a simple and cost-effective alternative: purchase a lease contract from one of the prestigious service portals for home, apartment and landowners on the internet. Here you will find something for very small money and can buy at each new lease a current version, which has been adapted by professionals to the current jurisdiction. On my website www.education-punk.de you will find some recommendations. Since the earning power of an apartment results from the cold rent, it is important when purchasing real estate to take a close look at this return on investment size. The decisive factors are: the type of lease, the "current lease" and the "future lease". With the "type of rental agreement" I want to point out the special case of the lump-sum rental contract in contrast to the usual standard rental agreement. The differentiation lies in the question whether both parties have agreed on a lump sum for operating costs or whether the operating costs of the dwelling are billed exactly to the extent of the expenditure. If both parties have agreed on a lump sum, this lump sum shall become due, irrespective of the actual development of the costs: If the additional costs increase, the landlord will lose. If the additional costs are reduced, the renter will lose. In retrospect, it can be stated on the basis of the continuous increase in costs: The landlord was the loser of this flat rate billing method. Accordingly, you should very well consider the purchase of a condominium with existing lump-sum lease.

The current lease: Mostly real estate is rented out: So, I buy an apartment with a tenant. Basically, the purchase in Germany does not break the lease. That means, by the purchase of the real estate the lease remains as it is. There is no special right of termination, but I enter with all rights and obligations in the lease as a landlord. One exception: If I wanted to use the apartment myself, but this should not be the case for investors.

Accordingly, it is important as a buyer to read the lease carefully. Not only the amount of the rent is essential, but also how the distribution of ancillary costs is regulated in the contract between tenant and landlord. The best regulation for the landlord is the one in which all recoverable additional costs are borne by the tenant. This type of contract provides that the user of the property bears the costs of use.

Important in the examination of the lease is also whether you as a buyer holds the right lease in your hands. Unfortunately, it happened to me that there were two lease versions: one that the tenant had and another that I had. My contract showed a higher cold rent than the tenant's contract. Thus, a higher profitability of the property was presented to me and then I falsely submitted a higher purchase price. So, I can only advise you to check the lease exactly. Let the seller show you the bank statements showing the rental incomes of the last three months. Check everything, even if you risk getting on the nerves of the real estate agent or the seller. People are creative in the sales process and you should simply put all the statements of the seller through their paces and make sure that you are not the victim of a marketing strategy in the end.

The future lease: This is about the question of whether the selected property will also be able to generate a good and stable net cold rent in the future. So it is about earnings expectations or the question of whether you can pay even in 10 or 20 years with the achievable rental income, the open credit commitments. You realize: It is a topic with consequences! Accordingly, you should not rely on the statements of the seller or the real estate agent, since statements about the future are mostly personal assessments. Other people are "valuable" whistleblowers. Ultimately, however, you should always inform yourself so as not to become the victim to a misjudgment of another human being. Basically, the best thing to do is to buy where you know the market well and as close as possible to where you live. So if I live in Nuremberg, for example, and I get an apartment, for example in Berlin - a foreign city to me - offered, then I rate the location fundamentally as a problem: There may be streets in Berlin, where the first street third is a luxury area, in the second third is a nice old buildings and in the third part live squatters. The problem: How should I as a non-local person correctly assess the real estate investment? Answer: Hard or only with a lot of time. In addition, I have to take on any object problem or a tenant change long journeys on me. This reduces my return and costs time, which I can use better elsewhere. Basically, for me: the further an investment is away from my place of residence, the worse I can assess and monitor it and vice versa.

This is also my basic logic in all investment projects: the less I understand something, the greater the likelihood that the project will be unprofitable for me. That's why I do not buy anything that I do not understand. So, I try to be an, "expert" in whatever I do - that is, to be as well informed as possible - and I acquire the knowledge that I lack by reading, or by getting advise by successful people in the way they proceed. For existing leases, you should pay attention to the rental deposit plus the fixed interest paid by the seller. Rental agreements with security deposit security are to be preferred.

The last test document in the rental contract check is the **handover protocol**. A handover protocol is the written documentation of the actual state of a rental property at the handover to the tenant. The record of damage and defects in the apartment may have been recorded, which already existed at the time of transfer / collection of the tenant. Accordingly, the protocol can provide us with valuable information regarding defects or damage that we have not yet noticed. In general, I would always recommend you as a landlord to create a handover protocol to settle on departure any detected damage that was not yet existing at the time of moving in with the tenant. Due to the change in the obligation to renovate on the side of the tenant when moving out (renovation is now the focus of the landlord) all damage caused by the tenant should be painstakingly recorded here. Also, I recommend carrying out the handover always in daylight, so that hard-to-see damage is better visible.

- **Construction and equipment description:** Especially in real estate financing, the financier usually requires a construction and equipment description. A corresponding template I have deposited for you as a free download on my website (www.education-punk.de). The construction and equipment description usually includes: General object information, construction, facade, roof and information on the expansion such as windows, floors, heating, plumbing and electrical installations.

- **Building insurance**: The building insurance is an insurance for the protection of buildings, outbuildings and garages. Basically, you can insure fire, line damage and natural hazards. Elemental damage is damage caused by the action of nature, such as storm, hail, earthquakes and floods. To secure the loan, financial institutions often require proof of building insurance. For this purpose and for your own protection, you should ask for proof before buying.

- **Land tax assessment**: The property tax is a tax on the ownership of land and its development. The landlord of a property can transfer the property tax of a residential property as part of the service charge settlement to the tenant. This tax is therefore for the landlord a continuous item. The tax assessment is the document in which the fixed property tax is shown by period and amount. Since the property tax is borne by the tenant, it plays a rather subordinate role for your return on investment calculation.

All the documents you receive from the seller, you do not need to gather yourself, if you want to sell someday. So, ask for as many documents as possible and more than maybe directly needed. It saves you work in the future and helps you to get the best possible impression of the object. In general, the seller likes to, because for him in the end the sale price as a "reward" beckons. My recommendation at this point: Let the seller work something for you. Create a separate folder for each object and place the documents there neatly. You will need the documents again and again. Here, initial good organization pays off.

6.3 The real estate agent — friend or foe

In times when the real estate market is booming and real estate seems to sell like sliced bread, you may wonder as a buyer why you even have to pay money for inconvenient services such as unlocking the front door or sending documents that the real estate agent got - mostly incomplete - from the owner. -. As a buyer, you would rather speak directly to the owner and save yourself "this postman". The reason for this is the seller, who wants to save time, talking to buyers, who then do not buy, or go through arduous negotiations. It also takes time to send documents or answer questions by post or e-mail.

As a result, the seller makes use of a service provider who makes his life easier and whose costs are added to the purchase price. Basically, the real estate agent has only one job to do: He is about as professional matching buyers and sellers together as in a dating agency. At the same time, the real estate agent tries to escape from any responsibility for what has been said and handed over through phrases like I have already read in various exposés: "The exposé was prepared on the basis of the documents pro-vided to us. We accept no liability for the accuracy or completeness."In my opinion, this situation needs to be changed. The one who orders the music should also pay for it. It would be a great improvement if the cost of the service provider had to be borne by the ordering seller alone. Of course, this could lead to the inclusion of this cost in the purchase price, but this purchase price would have to maintain competitive in the market and would not necessarily be considered as an evil by the buyer. The in-cidental acquisition costs, which from the point of view of the bank are not considered to be recoverable, would thereby be reduced and thus also a reduction in the use of equity capital. Of course, I do not want to say a negative word about the service quality of the real estate agent or this profession. They are sometimes important mediators and sellers, as well as experienced professionals, who are even absolutely crucial and indispensable regarding sales of complex objects. I'm just not a big fan of a system that does not give me as a buyer the option to choose whether to accept a particular service or not.

Basically, every buyer should consider all the information he receives from a realtor as: "selling points", because that's what they are. Accordingly, as a buyer, you should simply make sure that all information is corroborated by appropriate documents (evidence) so as not to go overboard to an over-motivated seller.

6.4 Searching for the right object

This chapter is about search strategies and is designed to help you find the cash flow deals that are needed for your successful asset accumulation. Since we are currently having a demand market in Germany for good real estate objects, so there is a lot of search competition and the search has become more time consuming. Experience has shown that you have to rate up to 100 objects to find the right one. That was different a few years ago.

The relationship between demand and supply changes over time and has many phases. Sometimes the market develops sideways, sometimes the supply is large and the demand is small and sometimes vice versa. Yet that is not bad, but serves you only as an indicator of your expected search effort. Sometimes the real estate search takes a few weeks and sometimes it takes just one year. As a rule, you are also not able to acquire a new object every three months. Accordingly, it is sufficient to find a suitable property once or twice a year. I recommend you to look at the whole thing like a hobby and to look at it with curiosity and desire to build wealth through as many objects as possible. With every visit you will learn something new and that is exactly what should be your long-term goal: learn something new and become better. Ultimately, your success is always determined by your knowledge. Real estate agents and sellers are often good teachers, both in a positive and a negative sense.

The most comfortably you can find object offers for you in the relevant real estate portals with free search jobs set, which then inform you automatically by e-mail about the results. So, you save the time-consuming search in portals and are conveniently informed about the latest object settings in your search category. On my service page www.education-punk.de you will find some real estate portals, which can help you to find your investment object.

A good search strategy is also to have a business card with the note "property investor" created. These can be scattered during visits with sellers, real estate agents and friends and thus build a long-term network of supporters and ad hoc advisors. It takes time, but it's not like you could buy an object every day. In times when I can not find suitable properties, I expand my equity base, improve my debt through special repayments or just enjoy the beautiful life. There are always opportunities. You just have to be patient. Fortune usually wanders from the impatient to the patient.

Foreclosures also provide the opportunity to make a good deal. Unfortunately, the auction dates are often overrun today, so that the property returns are eaten up by the impending rage of the impatient. Often, prices are paid that can not be achieved on the open market, as one or the other can be carried away by the competitive atmosphere of an auction to high bids. I myself have had little success in foreclosures so far. In addition, it is rarely possible to visit the object from the inside. You buy the property based on a synopsis. I do not like to buy a pig in a poke. As a very good strategy, it has proven to visit the tenant / still-owner of the condominium and ask if you can visit the apartment for an entrance fee of 50.00 or 100.00 €. That helps both sides. Another problem with foreclosures is the bank financing: Before each auction date you put the exposé before the bank, the bank checks the object, gives a promise or not, but you do not get the surcharge for the target price. If I have a good relationship with my bank, my banker will play the game a few times, but then the bank will usually intervene. The audit effort costs the bank money. Foreclosures are particularly suitable for people who are able to pre-finance the property entirely from own funds.

Looking for good return on investment objects with the help of property developers you can usually forget. These experts often know the real estate market so well that the purchase price is fixed to the maximum possible on the market. Accordingly, no positive cash flow remains for the investor. Also included in the calculation are very high rental income, capital gains and tax benefits, and each index is pulled to elicit attractive returns from the property. Often, the rental calculation is up to 40 percent above the regional rent index. Also, the return calculation is made without incidental acquisition costs, maintenance and repair costs and without consideration of non-recoverable costs. My experience is that you can definitely save conversations with developers, unless the developer has financial problems and needs to sell fast.

Real estate financing, for most buyers, involves contacting banks, credit intermediaries, building societies or insurance companies and usually causes discomfort because you have to move around on unfamiliar terrain where you do not feel well-educated. The best thing you can do in a foreign land is to get an overview in peace and not at the same time to sign a financing with the first one. Again, the golden rule for missing market overview applies: Always catch at least three offers. The real estate financing describes how the homebuyer finances the acquisition costs incurred with the acquisition of the property. However, in order to be able to decide on the best possible financing mix, the buyer must first determine the exact financing requirements or understand what costs can be incurred at all when buying a property. The acquisition costs essentially include the purchase price of the property plus incidental acquisition costs, which generally comprise the following components:

- **Costs of the realtor**: Of course, these costs only apply if the seller has commissioned a realtor to sell the property or if you are assisted by a realtor in the search (see chapter "7.3 The realtor - friend or foe"), The remuneration of a German real estate agent is usually in a corridor between 0 and 6 percent of the selling price plus the currently applicable value added tax. A distinction is made between internal and external commissions. Internal commission is what the seller gets charged by the real estate agent and external commission is what the real estate agent will charge you directly, in to, however, not more than 6 percent net. A common distribution is 3 percent inside and 3 percent outside commission. In some cases, an additional payment agreement is also fixed between the seller and the real estate agent. The seller specifies a target price. If the real estate agent achieves a higher selling price on the market than the target price, then the surplus proceeds belong to the real estate agent. This case is rather the exception; the rule is a commission agreement. Today, the majority of real estate is offered through real estate agents, as it is comfortable for the seller and costs "nothing". The seller waits until the real estate agent presents the pre-qualified buyer and then selects the desired candidate.

- **Real property transfer tax:** This tax rate is based on the tax rate established in the respective federal state and currently amounts to 3.5 to 6.5 percent of the purchase price for the property. In addition to the land, the components of a property also include the objects that are firmly connected to the land.
  When calculating the property tax, there is no need to take into account: movable property that is not an integral part of the property, such as the inventory (purchased fitted kitchen and other furniture) and reserves made from the housing allowance, which are attributable to the object of purchase.
  Accordingly, it is important to list these items in detail in the purchase contract so that these items / reserves can be deducted when calculating the real estate transfer tax. If these are not listed separately, experience shows that there is no deduction, because from where should the tax authorities know that a fitted kitchen is in your new apartment and what value this fitted kitchen has. Accordingly, a careful approach is worth money here. Another advantage regarding having a detailed breakdown (price and object) is that they usually have a shorter depreciation period than the proportion of buildings and so you have through a shorter depreciation period further tax advantages that should not be foregone carelessly.

- **Notary fees:** Every real estate purchase in Germany must become notarized. Accordingly, the visit to the notary is unavoidable. The task of the notary is the certification of legal transactions and the notary is indebted to independence and impartiality, which makes it especially for inexperienced homebuyers an important source of information. So, do yourself a favor and let the notary explain all text passages, which you do not understand. You can be sure that you get a fair and neutral information here. However, if you do not ask, then the notary gives his Latin translation as a "quick speaker" greatest honor and will recite the contract at full throttle. Here too, the motto is: time is money. I have often seen it at notary appointments that no one dares to ask, just to leave no "stupid" impression and when finally someone dared to ask, the rest of the round was also revealed as a non-knowledgeable. On my first notarized purchase contract, I did not understand much myself and – I think – I pretty annoyed the notary. But I prefer to leave an ignorant impression, than to be at the end the stupid one. Bad shame is not helpful here. So, let's explain the purchase contract completely and explain text modules that are incomprehensible to you. The services of the notary are currently consolidating at a cost of around 1.6 percent of the purchase price. The interest rate can vary. The best way to know the exact costs is to call the notary of choice.

As a result, the acquisition costs of a property are as follows:

Figure 21: Calculation of acquisition costs.

Purchase price:	100,000.00 €
Real estate agent commission (3% + VAT):	3,570.00 €
Land transfer tax Bavaria (3.5%): /Kitchen: 3.000,00 € /Reserves for renewal and replacement: 2,500.00 € (100,000.00 € - 3,000.00 € - 2,500.00 € = 94,500.00 €)	3,307.50 €
Notary costs (1.6%):	1,600.00 €
Total acquisition costs:	108,477.50 €

The ancillary acquisition costs for this sample property amount to around 8.50 percent of the purchase price. Without the use of a real estate agent and without deduction of inventory and maintenance reserve, the subordinate value would be 5.10 percent for the incidental acquisition costs. In a federal state with a high real estate transfer tax (6.50 percent) and with a maximum real estate agent external commission (7.14 percent), you then come to additional acquisition costs of 15.24 percent.

> **Note:** Incidental acquisition costs range from 5.10 percent to 15.24 percent of the purchase price.

Accordingly, the ancillary acquisition costs have a significant impact on the property return on investment and should not be forgotten in the return on investment calculation! According to my personal experience, real estate offers for investors, who have a return ratio, systematically forget the additional costs. So always calculate yourself and do not rely on representations of sellers. Before we come to the various financing concepts, we get to know our financing partner and his way of thinking better. The aim is to achieve optimum preparation for the financing discussion with the bank. Following the principle: Good preparation paves the way to success!

7.1   The bank's perspective as financier

"Take a hundred steps in someone else's shoes if you want to understand him," suggests an Indian proverb.

So slip into your banker's shoes. Please do not think about paint or hand-made leather shoes. It's about changing perspective. The goal is to understand why the one gets money from the bank and the other does not. Because only if I clearly recognize the difference, I will be able to prepare accordingly and to give my banker exactly what he needs to classify me and my property as creditworthy. It is therefore about putting oneself in the position of the interlocutor. The goal is to understand him and his way of thinking and then behave in such a way that the interlocutor puts me and my real estate project in the box in which I want to be stuck.

My experience here is quite clear: Basically, a bank as a private enterprise is interested in lending money. Nevertheless, making money only makes sense if you get your money back. That means: lending money means trust.

So you have to ask yourself in which case your bank considers you to be trustworthy and in which case not. In any case, the bank needs a basis of trust in order to be able to trust you. This basis of trust is formed by your "financial certificate" and the valuation of your property.

The fact is that in a bank conversation I have never been asked for my school report. Nor did I have the impression that my banker was particularly interested in the grades from my school years or the university. But what interests the bank is my "financial testimonial," which is carefully checked on every loan request. And with a bad "financial testimonial" I have as little chance of an interest-rate loan as a pupil would have on his dream job. The only problem is that many people do not even know their "financial record" or even know that there is such a thing as a "financial record". Accordingly, no effort is made to achieve good grades, although good grades would pay off especially here. It is therefore important to seek a good "financial record" before asking the bank for a real estate loan. A good certificate is not only useful for applying for a low-interest property loan but can also positively influence your dealings and your attitude to money. The "financial certificate", which can also be called a personal credit rating, consists of various parts, which are briefly described below:

- **Schufa score:** Schufa Holding AG (www.meineschufa.de) is a kind of "data collector" whose purpose is to gather information about economic entities in order to consolidate them and sell them to their owners and / or third parties. With an equity stake of over 80 percent, you could argue that the Schufa is owned by banks and savings banks. It is therefore primarily a sub-service provider for financial institutions and has the task of determining the creditworthiness of economic agents. So, data about you is collected and summarized into a credit score. This score is a numerical value between 100 and 1 percent and is used for risk classification. 100 percent is the best value. In addition to your contact details, usually any form of credit and leasing contracts, account openings, credit cards, telecommunication contracts, customer accounts in the field of trade / mail order, deviant payment behavior, submission of affidavits, arrest warrant for the execution of affidavits, opening of private insolvency proceedings, labor seizures, credit cards recorded in settlements, foreclosures and loan requests are recorded. Negative Schufa entries usually lead to a loan cancellation. For example, a negative entry could be an unpaid telecommunication bill. Even when determining a negative Schufa record in the computer system, the bank administrator has sometimes no way to even enter the loan request. So, the loan often ends before it started with the negative Schufa entry.

The key question is: what can you do to improve your financial record? Very few people know that they have a right to self-assessment. This means that once a year I can assert my rights and get to know which personal data (for example from Schufa) were stored about me. If there are wrong data stored about me, I can request the deletion of this data and thus eliminate even negative features. If there is information in your Schufa record that you can not handle money and have built your life on a par, this is a good place to start to change your life and thus improve your Schufa score. Any small improvement can, at best, lead to a better interest rate. You should definitely avoid consumer credit, because it clearly shows that you are unable to pursue goals with discipline. Certain emergency situations are of course excluded. But basically, the use of consumer credit, even in emergency situations, shows that I did not calculate it in advance; because there are always "emergencies" in life. The additional interest payments and monthly repayments also reduce the future financial scope. Often residual debt insurance and similar liaison credits are used to achieve effective returns that quickly make me pay 20 to 30 percent more for my apartment screen TV than if I just had to wait and save a bit. Thus, the alleged bargain is often a bad deal. Of course, I can well understand that you are fast becoming a victim of marketing. Unfortunately, with many things, short-term seduction is in direct conflict with long-term fulfillment. In my opinion, it is much more pleasant to first save voluntarily and then to consume than to first consume and then to be "forced" to save. I think you have got the picture.

- **Account management:** In addition to the consent to Schufa information we give the bank - if it is not already the house bank - our approval that information about us may be obtained from our house bank. This bank information contains information about our economic circumstances, our payment behavior and our business practices. In my personal experience, there are certain behaviors that banks are not particularly fond of and that should be avoided. I have picked out three of them:

01: "Submarine account management": The first culprit is best explained by the concept of a "submarine account manager". Each month after receiving cash, these people appear for a short time with their bank accounts on the credit side, befor the immediately submerge again into the depths of the disposition frame until the next month. Overdraft facilities are usually the most expensive loans available from a bank or savings bank and, with long dives, quickly vaporize a bigger part of your salary due to the interest costs. If these dives are too long and exceed a certain time window, it may even happen that your bank asks if you ran aground with your submarine. Submarine captains do not get good marks. As a rule, "overflights with occasional water landings" are rated better. Here is my recommendation: Stay away from long dives. If I can not shake off the diving, even the conversion to a pure credit account or a reduction of the overdraft facilities would be advisable, so that my submarine has virtually not the opportunity to dive.

02: **Overdrafting of the overdraft facilities**: The overdraft of the overdraft facilities granted not only leads to a higher overdraft interest rate but is usually rewarded with a special criticism in the certificate, which states that the account manager regularly exceeds the overdraft facilities granted. Simply put: The account manager can not handle money. That should be avoided in any case.

03: **Return debit due to lack of funds**: It is also not in your favor, if you allow third parties to collect amounts from your account by direct debit, without paying attention to the available balance. As a result, amounts can not be paid due to insufficient funds. That makes the bank do extra work and costs extra fees. The problem is that you show with this behavior that you don't have any overview of your finances. And that impacts your score. I was once given this information - but I'm sure that any financial institution handles it differently — but after three chargebacks per year you will get no more credits from your house bank. So, you should make sure that you do not generate return debit, if you want to have a good report.

- **Income situation:** The own income situation plays of course also a role in real estate financing. Accordingly, the homebuyer must submit a self-assessment in case of bank financing. This self-report consists of different sections. The section "income / expenditure situation" compares the income streams (e.g. income from employment, income from leasing and renting, income from self-employment, …) to total private expenditure. If you are interested in a good certificate, you should make sure that your monthly income is higher than your monthly expenses. Consumer loans, insurance, auto finance, expensive rental housing and subscriptions of any kind quickly ensure that income is consumed. The larger the revenue coverage, the better the grades and the higher the likelihood that you will get the loan you want. The topic of security is important for the lender: With a monthly financial surplus, the customer can bridge any special payments, repairs or short-term vacancies. So it's important that you keep track of your income and expenses on a regular basis and make sure that your monthly revenue surplus is positive. On my website: www.education-punk.de you can download for free a sample Excel template to keep track of your income and expenses.

Another part of self-disclosure is the balance sheet. The balance sheet is a list and comparison of your asset positions and liabilities. Again, the simple rule applies: liabilities are more likely to be disadvantageous and asset positions to be beneficial. But loans whose purpose is to build asset positions are not a sign that you are living beyond your means. An existing large fortune is not a prerequisite for real estate financing. According to experience, in Germany the bank demands a collateral or an equity investment of 20 percent of the purchase price plus the coverage of the incidental purchase costs. The better your financial report, the sooner the bank is ready to give you equity. On the website www.education-punk.de you can download for free a sample Excel template on the topic balance sheet. I recommend you to check your balance sheet in advance. If you identify potential for improvement, you can take appropriate precautions to put yourself in a good light at the bank. Here, too, the rule applies: People who are well prepared are usually successful. So check your financial record and get good grades. This will make your visit to the bank a success.

As every student knows, a report is only really good if there are no negative outliers and the grade point average is right. Basically, the better the certificate, the happier the walk to the bank. The beauty of the financial report is that, with a bit of discipline, everyone can earn a 1-A certificate.

7.2 Financing models at a glance

This chapter deals with the question: "How to finance the wealth accumulation with real estate in the best possible way?" The answer to this question not only puzzles inexperienced investors, but also always challenges "professional" real estate investors. Because investing in a property and its financing form a unit that should add up to a meaningful whole. So what is a meaningful financing? For me, this is a financing that

- generates a positive cash flow right from thr start,
- helps to build wealth,
- generates good returns,
- requires little equity and
- is safe and structured.

In accordance with the equity investment, this is called full or partial financing. If you finance the purchase costs to 100 percent over a loan, it is spoken of full financing. As soon as you bring in your own money, i.e. use equity capital, this is called a partial financing. The equity investment can be made in cash or through secondary securities, which then simply replaces the own contribution. For example, a life insurance or a partially / fully paid apartment can be used as secondary securities. Using the example of our sample property, the different types of financing would look as follows:

Purchase price:	92,000.00 €		
	Debt	Equity	Secondary security
Full financing	92,000.00 €	0.00 €	None
Partial financing	75,000.00 €	17,000.00 €	None
Full financing with securities	92,000.00 €	0.00 €	Other apartment or life insurance

As you have already learned, full financing is associated with increased risk for both the borrower and the lender. Accordingly, it is difficult to bring a bank to full funding. Experience has shown that exceptions are only possible if the borrower's financial report is above average and / or if secondary securities can be offered. The general disadvantage of full financing is that the cash flow is reduced by the higher monthly loan repayment. This increases the risk that the loan can no longer be serviced reliably in the event of liquidity bottlenecks. My maxim is: Safety first. Accordingly, in our sample property, we assume that we bring equity and partially finance the property.

Now the question arises as to which financing types are best used to finance the required debt. Here are primarily two types of financing usual, which are briefly presented below. On the presentation of the repayment loan is deliberately omitted, since it is not offered in practice by many insurance companies and building societies. We also neglect the possibility of foreign currency loans or Euribor financing, since these types of financing entail risks as well as some advantages.

- **Financing Type 01:** Final maturity (repayment-free) loan, backed by a financial contract. A bulletloan is a loan in which the loan amount is due only at the end of the term (full repayment at the end). During the loan period only, the interest is to be served (constant interest payments). With a fixed interest rate, the debt service thus consists of constantly high interest payments, as the following chart documents:

Figure 23: Graphical representation of a bullet loan.

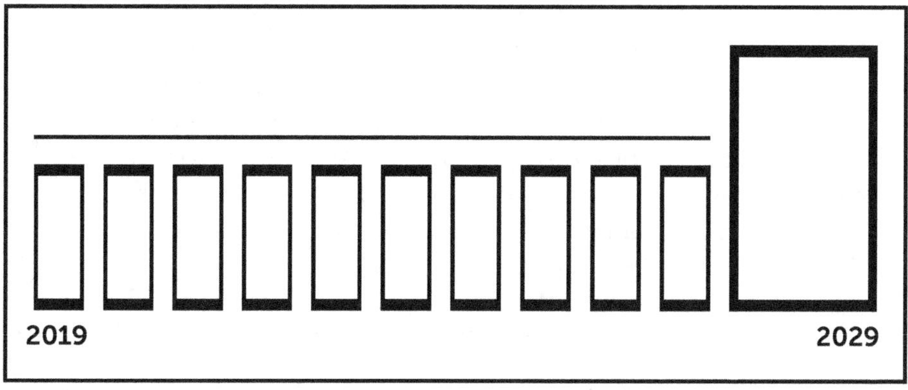

The repayment and saving of home loan savings contracts, endowment life insurance or investment funds is usually considered as repayment. They are combined with the bullet loan at maturity, so that the loan can be redeemed at the repayment date at the time of the due date of the loan. If not enough amortization has been saved in the amortization replacement, the balance will be refinanced and the game will start again from scratch until the loan is fully repaid. In the past, these forms of amortization replacement have received much criticism. Life insurance and fund saving plans have routinely generated lower effective return on investments compared to the lending rate of the bullet loan, often placing the borrower in much worse shape than a simple annuity loan. The problems with building society savings in turn are the high closing fee and the interest in the savings phase, which is often low, so on the bottom line you put more in it. Furthermore, the timing of the allocation of the home savings is unreliable, so it can happen that you have to finance it expensively. I'd rather know exactly what I have to pay each month than to be surprised by the result after 10 years. Surprises represent a deficit of control and a lack of control means increased risk. Accordingly, I am not a big fan of bullet loans.

- **Financing Type 02**: Fixed-rate mortgage/ Annuity Loan: In the case of an annuity loan, the amount of the monthly repayment payable remains constant throughout the agreed term. The interest rate is fixed for the corresponding period. The monthly repayment, also known as annuity, is made up of repayment and interest. Since the monthly repayment is continuously reduced by the residual debt, the interest portion in favor of the amortization portion also decreases along the way, as the following graph shows:

Figure 24: Graphical representation of a fixed-rate mortgage.

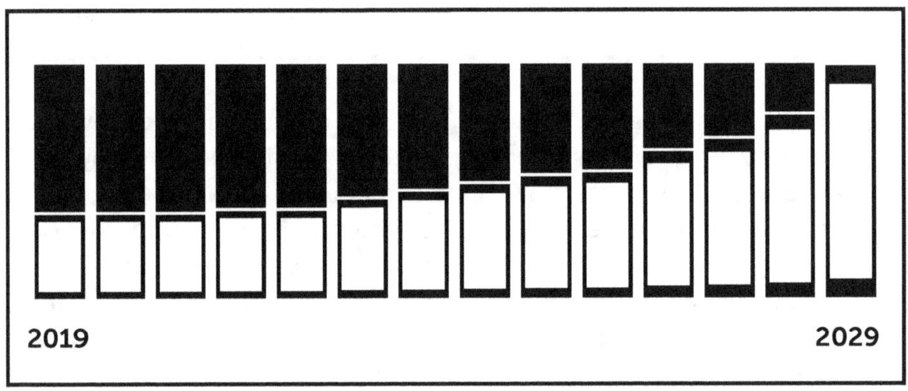

The annuity loan is one of the most common types of loans in Germany. The usual fixed interest periods in Germany are five, ten or fifteen years. Especially in the financing of the property-investment-triangle (liquidity, safety and return) should be placed in the focus of consideration. The focus here is on choosing a combination of financing form, type and duration, including possible loss of employment, possible problems with tenants, higher special charges or repairs, decline in real estate prices or increase in financing costs (rising interest rates at the moment of follow-up financing) does not generate unnecessarily high risk. A real estate investment should be designed as an independent freelancer who works for you and your asset accumulation. Accordingly, some basic rules should be taken into account when funding:

- **Form of financing**: In practice, an equity ratio of 20 percent of the acquisition costs has proven to be a good starting point. This equity ratio fulfills several functions: For the bank, the equity interest represents additional security in addition to the property to be acquired. Banks usually charge a discount of 20 to 40 percent of the market value of the property. This value is also called collateral value and is based on a separate valuation of the financial institutions. The mortgage collateral value is the value that credit security represents for the lender. This collateral value is often the upper limit up to which a financial institution can grant loans. It is a value that can most likely be expected to be realized on the market over the long term and at any time.

  Using equity reduces your monthly financing, as you have to borrow less to finance the property. Accordingly, your specific investment risk will be reduced, as there may not be a potentially threatening situation (due to higher monthly repayment charges) if property prices fall or if interest rates rise at the time of follow-up financing. In addition, your interest rate conditions / bargaining position at the financial institutions improve with the increase in equity, as the default risk for the banks is reduced with a higher equity capital contribution. The monthly cash outflow is essentially determined by the financing concept of the real estate, i.e. a small annuity rate ensures little cash outflow and vice versa.

- **Financing type and maturity**: My favorite is an annuity loan with 1 percent repayment and 10 percent special repayment with a maturity between ten and fifteen years. This form of financing combines flexibility - with the possibility of annual special repayment - with a low monthly burden (security). This combination can usually mitigate problems such as changes of tenant, payment difficulties of the tenant or surprising special payments and repairs. If you want to keep the property for the long term, you can easily finance it in the long run. Long maturities reduce the risk of rising monthly payments with an increase in the general interest rate level. Accordingly, I finance for at least ten years. In addition, I consistently use the positive cash flow (cash surplus) for special repayments. Otherwise, there is a risk that a repayment rate of one percent will "never" repay the property. Here, discipline is needed again.

With favorable interest rates, loan terms of more than ten years are also worthwhile. In Germany, the borrower has a one-sided special termination right for terms of more than ten years. Private borrowers may terminate the loan agreement with a notice period of six months from the tenth year after full receipt of the loan (§489 BGB (German Civil Law) - ordinary termination right of the borrower). So should the general interest rate levels fall, you as a borrower can terminate your loan early and renegotiate the contract. If the interest rate has risen, then you simply stay with your old loan agreement and continue to service it. For loan contracts, the motto is: the longer, the safer. However, you pay for a longer interest rate usually a higher interest rate. Conversely, the advantage of a short-term fixed interest rate is the lower interest rate and thus a lower monthly rate. However, a short-fixed interest rate usually only pays off if the loan can be repaid quickly through high special repayments. Otherwise, the risk increases that the interest rate level will increase in the meantime and the follow-on financing will become more expensive. So, if you can not repatriate your loan in a short time - which should be the rule - then rather choose a longer fixed interest rate.

I primarily use classic annuity loans myself, which I would also recommend to you. I am a friend of minimum repayment (1 to 2 percent). This leaves me more money and I am not forced to subsidize the objects on a monthly basis. I do not like bulletloans because of the "insecure" repayment substitutes, such as home loan savers, endowment life insurance or investment funds. For me, this is quite simple: Everything that makes the financing more complex, I experience, returns and is at the expense of a reliable calculability. I would also not recommend to finance a property with a partner. Experience has shown that this reduces the creditworthiness of both borrowers: The loan repayment is fully charged to both partners and the rent is only credited to 50 percent each. Moreover, in practice, it is difficult to have one of the two borrowers removed from the loan agreement, as this increases the lender's risk. And who actually likes a risk increase or return on investment decrease.

In addition to the purchase of real estate and financing, the amount and reliability of the rental payments primarily determine whether or not you have acquired a "cash machine" with your real estate purchase. Accordingly, with the selection of the object, the financing and the choice of the tenant, the return on investment of the property is defined. Bearing so much responsibility can make you nervous too. On the other hand, it gives you the control to turn a real estate investment into a success. At this point again, a very clear advice: The selection of real estate and the selection of the tenant should **never** be completely delegated to third parties. The last decision you should always take yourself. Only when you have developed a good sense of proportion through experience, you can assign these topics to third parties. But you should not give up having a personal look at the tenant before you go to the notary or agree to a tenant. A bad selection delays asset accumulation.

Before we think about what kind of tenant we are looking for, we have to ask ourselves: what do we want under no circumstances? The answer is clear: we do not want surprises, surprises and surprises. Rent failures, delayed payments, harassment of other residents (for example due to noise, smell, smoke and vandalism) and having to pay the deposit are surprises that I would like to avoid.

A good tenant selection is only possible if there is also a selection of tenants. In other words, the more special the property is and the smaller the market for buyers, the smaller the opportunity to find the best possible tenant. This means that the risk increases when there are only a few prospective tenants. Then I either do not rent at all or have to take the present tenant. Since we have learned which properties are interesting for us and have therefore made the right choice, we can be sure that we will have enough potential tenants to choose from with one simple ad.
How does the optimal tenant look like? Only if I know exactly who I want, I can also look for the right person. In doing so, I came across the following

criteria, which build for me a good relationship between tenant and land-lord: I prefer a long-term tenancy based on mutual harmony. I do not like constant changes of tenants and no constant entries and exits. The completion of transfer protocols is a horror to me and I do not want to explain the benefits of the apartment constantly to potential tenants. I' look for a reliable long-term tenant. I do not want stress and no extra work. I look for a comfortable way to earn money.

If you decide to hire a real estate agent for the rental, you should formulate clear rules and requirements when choosing the right tenant. After all, the real estate agent is not paid to let the tenant pay his rent, but to get you a prospective tenant. The landlord suffers from a bad tenant selection. Of course, there are also good real estate agents on the market. But a little distrust never hurts. That prevents bad surprises. So always keep your eyes open when changing tenants!

Note: We look for the stress-free long-term tenant!

Please also forget the image of the terrible landlord, who ignores every problem of his tenants and collects high rents. The whole thing should function like a small and friendly business relationship. Problems are discussed and solutions are found that are acceptable to both parties. Apartment defects are resolved as soon as possible. If there is damage, the person who caused the problem will be liable for it. If there is normal wear and tear, I pay the bill as a landlord. If the tenant wants an individual housing modernization, then I will finance it - if I can - and I agree in writing with the tenant for a rent increase, because for him, the living comfort will be higher. It is not about the fact that one side gains more than the other, but that the deal is fair. Only then, as a landlord, you have the chance of a good landlord-tenant relationship. But it is important that we do not let ourselves be fooled. Accordingly, there are the following criteria that are important in the selection of a tenant:

- The rent is always paid on time and at the latest by the third in advance for the following month.
- The security deposit is to be made at / before the lease is signed (no rental deposit means no lease).
- If there are any problems with the property, the tenant will contact you immediately and reliably in order to be able to rectify any damage immediately.
- The tenant maintains a cooperative style of communication and addresses problems directly.
- If the tenant has financial problems and the rent comes a few days later, he immediately communicates that and tries to find a solution together with the landlord.
- The tenant handles the rental property with care. Best of all, as if it were his property and not thinking: "No need to be gentle, it is a rental property after all."
- The tenant prefers a friendly relationship with the landlord, who ensures that both sides treat each other with care, understanding and benevolence.
- The tenant stays as long as possible in the apartment, so that there are fewer tenant changes / relocations.

Now that we know the requirement profile, the question arises: How can I ensure that the potential tenant corresponds exactly to this profile? Here is where my experience as co-founder and authorized representative of a microfinance institute (www.mein-mikrofinanzierer.de) came in handy. Because when it comes to lending money the same profile of requirements applies: You lend a good - in the case of microfinance, a loan - and receive interest as a price for the loan. As a lender, you want to get your money back plus interest as reliably as possible and you do not want any stress, extra effort or issues. Likewise, when renting an apartment, you want to get a rental interest (old term for rent) and receive the property at the end of the term intact and without any damage. That is, the landlord is in principle the same as the banker. The only difference is that you as a landlord have no training for the subject of "rental" and you have to fight for your way by yourself. But do not worry: Help is coming up!

The same applies for lending. Accordingly, the same solution approaches are applicable to obtain the lowest possible "problem rate". For the selection of the tenant, I have got used to a special procedure with which I have succeeded so far. Since we have only a small window of opportunity during the interview with the prospective tenant, I take everything seriously. I interpret every little irregularity of the tenant. In other words, the behavior of the tenant before and during the initial conversation I see as his normal behavior. This is certainly not always fair, and I have certainly often wronged good tenants. However, this reduces the likelihood of having problems with your tenants and, after all, the prospective tenant has the opportunity to do well. Now here's my checklist for the tenant selection:

- **Consistent and fair:** Be consistent and fair to all prospective tenants and do not let yourself be begged or lulled!

- **Gut feeling factor:** One of the most important maxims of my selection: If the potential tenant has anything that I do not like, or if my gut tells me there is something weird about this person, then I'll never ignore that. That means: use your gut feeling. Do not try to figure out why you have a bad gut feeling. The fact is, there is nothing stupider than to admit to yourself that somehow you had a bad feeling from the beginning. The fact is: The apartment is yours, you have worked hard for it and you can do and leave what you want with your property, as long as you do not violate any laws and harm other people.

- **Behavior:** If the tenant is unpunctual or unreliable, I go straight to the next candidate. As a rule, reliable and punctual people are also reliable and punctual tenants and vice versa. There is a nice saying: The way you behave in the small, you behave in other things. So do not risk listening to excuses all the time. There is no need for it. Why settle for excuses, if there is probably another ideal tenant out there? You are the owner and you want to make money from your investment and that is legitimate. Even if you are a caring person and you want to help a disadvantaged person, who has been looking for a home for months, ask yourself the following questions: Why was the man not punctual, why did he not bring the complete documents and why does he not understand that he had to bring a Schufa information. Is the apartment important for him? If you want a reliable tenant, look for reliability. My personal experience in dealing with microcredits is: the human being that you encounter in the first meeting is often the same you will have to deal with later. There are always exceptions, but do you really want to search for this exception? Go the safest way possible and generally try to avoid surprises! That will give you a reliable rental flow within five or ten years.

- **Documents / information of the tenant:** The prospective tenant is not legally obliged to submit his documents. On the other hand, you as a landlord have freedom of contract and can refuse to conclude a lease without mentioning a reason. Accordingly, you can ask the prospective tenant for information and he can decide for himself which documents he would like to bring to the appointment and which not. Personally, I never choose a tenant I can not judge.

I ask prospective tenants for the following documents:

Self-disclosure form: The self-disclosure requests personal data regarding the prospective customer: marital status, number of members belonging to the household, smokers among the members or music in the home, contact details of the previous tenant, monthly net earnings, pets and possible bankruptcy or insolvency proceedings and dunning notices. This will give you a first good impression of who you are dealing with. A corresponding template can be found for free at: www.education-punk.de.

Curriculum vitae: A CV gives you a picture of the professional person we have in front of us. It shows if the potential tenant has often been unemployed, shows us the level of qualification with which the tenant enters the labor market and in which industry the tenant is employed to earn his living. A well-qualified tenant in a secure position is more likely to be our preferred candidate than a less-skilled tenant in a crisis industry who has often been unemployed. From the duration of the employment relationship conclusions can be drawn whether the tenant is still in the probationary period or whether he has already established a good and solid employment relationship with the employer. Temporary work should be treated with caution in this context, as employment through a temporary employment agency can quickly come to an end. Self-employed people should have worked successfully for at least three to five years. Instead of a salary slip I would ask for the last three financial statements (do not forget the stamp of the tax accountant or the accounting office).

Schufa self-disclosure: I ask every tenant to bring a Schufa self-disclosure. What function the Schufa information has when lending, you can read in chapter 8.1. For the landlord valuable information on the general payment and moving behavior becomes visible. Useful box thinking: We suggest that a tenant who does not pay his phone bill on time is more likely to pay his / her rent on time. If you discover negative entries - of any kind - and / or a Schufa total score of less than 88 percent, you should think twice about whether this tenant is the right one for you and in case of doubt, just keep searching. Because there is no reason to expose yourself to negative probabilities that can already be detected in advance. In other words, why do I want to get involved with a tenant who is likely to cause problems when there are alternatives? Of course, there are exceptions, but the question is always: Must / Should I really look for them? My personal recommendation: Recommend your prospective tenant to do his homework and clean-up his "financial testimonial". Then he can apply for the next rental with you. In practice, there is no reason not to clear up misunderstandings in the Schufa.

Long-term tenants: The Schufa also provides information about how often the tenant moved. Here usually the current and the last residence are listed. You can ask questions in the interview hereto. For example, how long have you lived there, why do you want to move now and how long do you plan to live here. Sometimes a bit of detective work is needed here to detect the "hidden intension", i.e. the hidden intentions of the tenant. Just take your time and ask carefully. It also makes sense to ask for the contact details of the last landlord in order to inquire whether the tenant has behaved reliably and problem-free. We are looking for a punctual, respectful and unproblematic person. If a witness tells you that your tenant has exactly those qualities, that's the best security.

The salary statement: The salary statement should confirm the information from the self-assessment and assure you that the net wage of the renter / tenant is sufficient to reliably pay the rent. The total rent including all ancillary costs should not exceed 30 to 40 percent of the net income. Because that means that the tenant can afford the rent well. The last three salary / pay slips should be submitted as proof of salary, or the annual accounts of the last three years for a self-employed person.

Copy of identity card: A copy of the identity card is used to identify the tenant, thus preventing any form of identity theft.

For tenants or students in need of care, you should always have a solvent relative sign as a direct guarantor in order to ensure a regular rental income. The same is true in any case for people, where you are not sure about the regular rental entrance. In shared apartments, each resident should enter as a tenant in the joint and several contract or sign the lease with.
This form of selection process might seem overly cautious at first sight, and that is exactly what it is, because we do not want to create any ground for negative surprises. You can download for free a checklist with all the necessary documents and a template for the tenant's self-assessment from www.education-punk.de so that the selection process is as easy as possible for you.

Now there are only my final words missing and I wish you much success with your wealth creation through real estate! If you still lack information or you find improvement options in my book, then I will be very happy about your feedback (www.education-punk.de). Because me, too, I still have much to learn and you can never know everything. Your feedback is highly appreciated!

9 Epilogue

One of the problems of guidebooks and articles is that they are often written by people who only have theoretical knowledge. I personally call this a eunuch knowledge. You know how it works, but you just have no practical experience. In the vernacular this group of people is also often referred to as a "mouth artisan". In the real estate sector, these would probably be people who write about the advantages and disadvantages of real estate investments, but who hardly own a handful or have ever owned one themselves. My recommendation at this point: Look for mentors or role models who are already where you want to be tomorrow. Exactly these people take you further and can tell you how the real estate business works. Many people dream of being able to live on their rental income, but they shy away from the training and experience that they have to go through to reach that goal. Grow with your experience, be disciplined and set yourself small achievable goals, which you then implement.

By writing this book, I did my best to present you my personal experiences in building up assets through real estate. The system I presented you might not be the only one, but it worked pretty well for me and I have developed it so that it can be used by everyone as a blueprint to build up fortune with real estate. I can assure you that I haven't received any gifts. Where I am today is the result of many years of hard work and I am proud of this!

Most people want results but aren't willing to put in the hard work that is required to achieve their goals. It is not about the money that makes you wealthy in the end; it is about the knowledge that you have acquired in the real estate business, as this enables you to start over and over again.

One reason why many people do not succeed is that they only want the result but are not prepared to do the work that is necessary to achieve what they want. It is important to know that it is not the money that makes you wealthy in the end, but the knowledge that you have acquired in the real estate sector and that enables you to start over and over again.

I wish you good luck!
Florian

Subject index

List of figures

Disclaimer

The author describes the development of a real estate asset from his own experience perspective and with conscientious examination of the market and legal situation at the time of first publication. The book offers decision support for the solution of typical questions in connection with real estate, but does not replace a critical examination of all questions and decision possibilities arising in connection with the construction of real estate assets in individual cases.

(All rights to this book belong to Education Punk ltd.
All figures used in this book are own illustrations.)

Notes

Notes

Notes